TWAYNE'S WORLD AUTHORS SERIES

A Survey of the World's Literature

Sylvia E. Bowman, Indiana University

GENERAL EDITOR

AUSTRALIA

Joseph Jones, University of Texas, Austin

EDITOR

Douglas Stewart

TWAS 327

Douglas Stewart

Douglas Stewart

By CLEMENT SEMMLER

Twayne Publishers, Inc.   ::   New York

Library of Congress Cataloging in Publication Data

Semmler, Clement.
    Douglas Stewart.

    (Twayne's world authors series, TWAS 327. Australia)
    1. Stewart, Douglas Alexander, 1913–   —Criticism and
interpretation.
PR9619.3.S8Z88   1974   821   74-7389
ISBN 0-8057-2863-5

821.91
5849S

For Cathy

I send this sheaf of roses and these colours,
That when the cream rose dies, the blue fire dims,
Remembering me, your cool soul may grow warm
As sunlight warms the moonlight of your limbs.

—Douglas Stewart, "With a Sheaf of Cream Roses"
(From *The White Cry*, 1939)

Contents

Preface

Acknowledgments

Chronology

1. Douglas Stewart's Place among His Contemporaries:

   An Introduction   15

2. Douglas Stewart as Poet   22

3. Douglas Stewart as Verse Playwright   59

4. Douglas Stewart as Prose Writer   114

5. Douglas Stewart as Editor/Critic   129

   Conclusion   152

   Notes and References   155

   Selected Bibliography   161

   Index   167

About the Author

Clement Semmler is one of Australia's best-known literary figures. Scholar, critic, anthologist, and biographer, he has had the singular honor of a Doctorate of Letters conferred on him by examination of his published work, which ranges from critical studies of James Joyce and modern Irish literature to Australian writers, such as Kenneth Slessor, Brian James and A. B. "Banjo" Paterson. He has been a principal literary reviewer of the *Sydney Morning Herald* for almost twenty years, is a frequent contributor to Australian literary journals, and is a consulting editor for *Poetry Australia*.

Dr. Semmler has had a distinguished career as a broadcaster and is the Deputy General Manager of the Australian Broadcasting Commission. He was awarded the Order of the British Empire in 1972 for his services to Australian literature and he occupies many distinguished positions in Australian public and educational life, including the Chairmanship of the Australian Immigration Publicity Council, membership of the Council of the New South Wales Public Library and of the Committee for the Humanities established by the Council of the Australian National Library, and of committees advisory to Australian universities and advanced Colleges of Education.

Dr. Semmler is the author of *For the Uncanny Man: Essays, Mainly Literary* (*on James Joyce and Others*), Melbourne, 1963; *Barcroft Boake: Poet of the Stockwhip,* Melbourne, 1965; *A. B. "Banjo" Paterson* ("Australian Writers and Their Work" series), Melbourne, 1965; *Kenneth Slessor* ("British Writers and Their Work" series), London, 1966; reprinted, 1969; 2nd Edition, 1974; *The Banjo of the Bush,* Sydney and London, 1966; reprinted, 1967; *A. B. Paterson* ("Great Australians" series), Melbourne, 1967; and *The Art of Brian James, and Other Essays on Australian Literature,* St. Lucia, 1972.

He has edited *Literary Australia* (with Derek Whitelock), Melbourne, 1965; *Stories of the Riverina,* Sydney, 1965; *Coast to Coast 1965–66* (Australian Short Stories), Sydney and London, 1966; *The World of Banjo Paterson,* Sydney and London, 1967; and *Twentieth Century Australian Literary Criticism,* Melbourne, 1967.

Preface

Douglas Stewart represents the establishment of Australian poetry, ranking with his contemporaries Judith Wright, A. D. Hope, R. D. FitzGerald, James McAuley and the late Kenneth Slessor as a major poet of his country.

Stewart is internationally known as a writer of radio verse plays: his *Fire on the Snow,* based on the epic of Scott's unsuccessful dash to the South Pole, has been broadcast in most countries of the Western world. The purpose of this study is first of all to show Stewart's remarkable versatility—for which he stands supreme among present-day Australian writers—not only as poet and playwright, but also as a short-story writer, essayist, and elegantly discerning literary critic. Furthermore, in his profession as literary, and later, publishing editor and anthologist he has been for over thirty years a continuing and stimulating influence on younger writers many of whom, now approaching maturity, have gratefully acknowledged their debt to him in their published work.

Secondly, this book attempts to relate in a proper perspective Stewart's achievement as one who has so remarkably brought poetry back into fashion. He has done this partly by his nature poetry, in which he is by far the best practitioner his country has yet produced: for him the visible world powerfully exists and he has set precisely and beautifully in his poetic amber, tender and elegiac evocations of the denizens of the Australian bush. But also in his scrupulous observation of the minutiae of creatures and things his poetic glance has broadened over the years so that the net of his inspiration has come to scoop in every experience where poetry had lurked undetected and unremarked. City traffic, possums in the roof, boys asleep on the beach, odd occasions in history, cows being milked, a silk-worm spinning its cocoon—all are transmuted into memorable speech, in forms which range from the lyric and the sonnet to the ballad (in which form Stewart is also preeminent among his peers). Yet his poetic style remains as explicit as it is melodic; as A. A. Phillips, one of Australia's most respected literary critics, has remarked, Stewart "sounds like a mid-twentieth century man of sensitive intelligence talking in easy communication with a friend." It is in this way especially that, as this study endeavors to show, he has spearheaded a wider appreciation of poetry in Australia.

CLEMENT SEMMLER

Sydney, Australia

Acknowledgments

I gratefully acknowledge the permission of Angus and Robertson Pty. Ltd. of Sydney, Australia, to quote extensively from Douglas Stewart's *Collected Poems 1936–1967*, *Four Plays*, *The Girl with Red Hair*, *The Flesh and The Spirit*, and *The Seven Rivers*. My friendship with Douglas Stewart himself has, I believe, survived my constant appeals to him for the checking of biographical and other facts of reference—and I am deeply appreciative of his unfailing patience and understanding. He too has agreed that I may quote from any of his poems.

Finally, I thank my ABC colleagues, Ruth Sullivan and Judith Clark, the Librarian of the ABC (and her staff), for their valued help. Willing and courteous assistance given me in the Mitchell Library of New South Wales is also warmly acknowledged.

Chronology

1913 Born in Eltham, Taranaki Province, New Zealand, May 6, 1913.

1919– Attended Eltham Public School.
1926

1926– Attended Plymouth Boys' High School.
1930

1930 Began studies at Victoria University, Wellington, New Zealand.

1931– Worked as journalist on New Zealand newspapers.
1932

1933 Came to Australia for brief period of free-lance writing. Returned to New Zealand and continued work as journalist/ writer.

1936 Published first book of verse, *Green Lions*, in Auckland, New Zealand.

1938 Traveled to England and then to Australia to become assistant to Literary Editor of *The Bulletin*.

1939 Published *The White Cry* (poems) in London.

1940 Appointed "Red Page" (i.e., literary) Editor of *The Bulletin*. Published *Elegy for an Airman* (poems) in Sydney.

1941 Published *Sonnets to the Unknown Soldier* (poems) in Sydney. *The Fire on the Snow* first verse-play broadcast on networks of Australian Broadcasting Commission.

1943 Published *Ned Kelly*, a play, in Sydney.

1944 Published *The Fire on the Snow* and *The Golden Lover* (two plays for radio) in Sydney. Published *The Girl with Red Hair* (short stories) in Sydney.

1946 Married Australian artist Margaret Coen on December 5. Published *The Dosser in Springtime* (poems) in Sydney.

1947 Published *Glencoe*, a series of ballads, and *Shipwreck*, a poetic drama, in Sydney.

1948 Daughter, Margaret Mary Elizabeth, born in Sydney. Published *The Flesh and the Spirit: An Outlook on Literature*, in Sydney.

1952 Published *Sun Orchids* (poems) in Sydney.

1954 Awarded UNESCO traveling scholarship.

1955 Published *The Birdsville Track and Other Poems* in Sydney. Published *Australian Bush Ballads* (which he coedited with Nancy Keesing) in Sydney. Appointed to Advisory Board of Commonwealth Literary Fund.

1957 Published *Old Bush Songs and Rhymes of Colonial Times* (which he coedited with Nancy Keesing) in Sydney.

1958 Published his four most successful verse-plays (*The Fire on the Snow, The Golden Lover, Ned Kelly, Shipwreck*) under the title of *Four Plays*, Sydney.

1960 Awarded Order of the British Empire. Left *The Bulletin* and joined the Sydney publishing firm of Angus and Robertson as a Literary Editor. Published *Fisher's Ghost* (an historical comedy), Sydney. Published *Voyager Poems*, which he edited and in which he included some of his poetry.

1962 Published *The Garden of Ships* (a poem), Sydney. Published *Rutherford and Other Poems*, Sydney.

1963 Published *Douglas Stewart: Selected Poems*, which he selected and for which he contributed an Introduction, Sydney.

1964 Published *Modern Australian Verse*, which he edited and for which he chose the poems included, Sydney.

1965 The above selection, under the same title, was published by the University of California Press, Berkeley.

1966 Published *Hugh McCrae: Selected Poems*, which he edited with an Introduction. Published *The Seven Rivers*, illustrated by his wife, Margaret Coen, Sydney.

1967 Published *The Pacific Book of Bush Ballads*, which he edited, Sydney. Published *Short Stories of Australia: The Lawson Tradition*, which he selected and to which he contributed an Introduction, Sydney. Published *Collected Poems 1936–1967*, which he selected, Sydney.

1968 Received Britannica Australia Award in the Humanities ($10,000).

CHAPTER 1

Douglas Stewart's Place among His Contemporaries: An Introduction

I *His Versatility*

WHEN she began her short study of Douglas Stewart,[1] Nancy Keesing, herself a poet, editor, and critic of considerable standing in Australian letters, was moved to write: "Douglas Stewart is the most versatile writer in Australia today —perhaps the most versatile who ever lived in this country. He is a poet whose poetry and nature as a poet are central to everything in which he excels."

It is a correct and proper assessment. He is among the foremost of Australian poets, ranking with Judith Wright, A. D. Hope, R. D. FitzGerald, and James McAuley as the best of his generation, but distinct from them because the subject matter of his poetry covers a wider range. He is less concerned with abstract and philosophical themes and more concerned with landscape, achievement, and history. He yields to no contemporary Australian poet as a lyricist. As a playwright, he became the only Australian who has placed himself internationally as a radio verse dramatist and has had the distinction of having had his radio plays broadcast in over twenty countries. It was his example as a dramatist in the 1940s that was one of the major factors prompting the subsequent renascence of post–World War II Australian writing for the theater. In short, as the historian and critic Geoffrey Serle in a 1973 study (*From Deserts the Prophets Come: The Creative Spirit in Australia 1788–1972*) has described Stewart, he is "the great all-rounder of modern Australian literature."[2]

He was literary editor of the Australian *Bulletin* from 1940 for over twenty years and molded the talents of many young

writers by his example and guidance. Later, in Australian publishing, he was to edit a string of anthologies which have
become basic texts for the evaluation of Australian literature
in this and the last century. He combined with his editing
activities the writing of literary criticism that is at once a
significant and valuable part of his output. In his writing career
he has also published many short stories that are distinctive
in flavor and style as well as many general essays that are
charming and unusual in their subject matter.

II *Richness of Background*

It may well be argued that this astonishing versatility may
be traced to the fact that Stewart is, or has been, a citizen of
two countries—of New Zealand and Australia; and these different
backgrounds of experience (and indeed their similarities) have
given Stewart a rich storehouse for his literary proclivities,
providing him with an extraordinary variety of literary motifs.
It is worthwhile considering these backgrounds in some detail,
toward an understanding of Stewart as a writer.

He was born in Eltham, New Zealand, in 1913, the son of
an Australian of Scots descent who practiced as a lawyer in
that town. His father, who preserved a great love for his native
country, subscribed to *The Bulletin,* and from his regular reading
of it young Douglas became interested in Australian lore and
legends and the mysterious attraction which this much larger
country offered. The young Stewart accompanied his father on
the latter's several trips to Australia to see his family and formed
some ideas himself of this larger and unusual land. In the
meantime he went as a boarding student to New Plymouth
Boys' High School (which was about thirty miles from where
he lived) and then to the University in Wellington, where he
began to study law, but soon abandoned the study in favor of
writing and journalism.

Stewart loved the New Zealand countryside. He went often
for holidays among its picturesque mountains, valleys, and
streams. He thus acquired an enthusiasm for nature in all its
forms and in the process became an enthusiastic fisherman. He
began work as a journalist on local country newspapers and

by this time was writing poetry, short stories, and essays for both Australian and New Zealand periodicals and journals.

After a short visit to Europe, he came to Australia in 1938 to make his permanent home there, and soon after he began his twenty years' association with *The Bulletin*. He became friends with Australian writers of the period, among them Ronald McCuaig, Cecil Mann, R. D. FitzGerald, Hugh McCrae, Kenneth Mackenzie, and the artist Norman Lindsay, with whom eventually he formed a lifetime's friendship. It was through an introduction by Mackenzie that he met the poet Kenneth Slessor, which also led to a warm and lasting friendship. It is important to stress, however, that Stewart admits to the influence of none of these writers: he takes an individualist's pride in the distinctiveness of his own writing.

III   *Preeminence as a Nature Poet*

Stewart in the many fluent forms his poetry has taken reached particular eminence as Australia's foremost nature poet. Indeed, from the time of his arrival in Australia he began to explore the Australian countryside with the same passionate interest of his New Zealand wanderings. In particular he roamed the mountain areas of the Southeastern part of Australia—the Snowy Mountains region—which along with his visits to the Blue Mountains and other country areas of New South Wales gave subject matter and themes to much of his poetry and prose writing, and also gave ample scope and variety for his hobby of fishing. His growing love for the Australian bush helped to foster his interest in the Australian ballad (on which he was to become one of his country's most knowledgeable authorities).

Nancy Keesing makes an interesting observation about the "counterpoise" of Stewart's New Zealand and Australian backgrounds. In his earlier Australian writings—his plays and poetry particularly—while there is great "breadth and gusto" in his handling of Australian themes, there is not the intricate and experienced detail of his early New Zealand writing. But there emerged gradual changes in Stewart's descriptive emphasis as between the two countries.

As he explored Australia, perceiving and assimilating its smaller features, learning the names and habits of plants and animals, so his poems, as book succeeded book, mirrored his growing love and delight in fine details. But he returned periodically to New Zealand themes, and as his Australian vision became gradually more particular, so his New Zealand view became correspondingly more general. In the *latest* New Zealand poems, like "Rutherford" and "Tanemahuta," the descriptive writing has a great, vigorous sweep whose closest affinities are with the Australia of *Ned Kelly* or "Black Opal."[3]

IV *General Approach to Poetry*

One can add, of course, that this view must be related to the sweep of Stewart's poetic imagination toward historical and general themes. He is the last poet who would retreat into his ivory tower, so to speak; rather he believes[4] (because he admires the earlier Australian writers who did this very thing) that in a new country, the motivation of its voyagers and explorers must be examined; the domestic mythology of the country must be probed; there must be a search for the truths of the earth—a discovery and assessment of the environment, as it were, by means of nature poetry; there must be a willingness by Australian writers as with any writers in a "new" country to take advantage of the fresh subject matter thrown in their way. All this, of course, Stewart has done—from verse plays like *Ned Kelly* and *Shipwreck* to his nature poems about Australian birds, flowers, and animals, and such a sequence of poems about the Australian desert country as *The Birdsville Track*. Stewart has no doubt that "this newness, this feeling of discovery, has helped to produce some of the finest poetry that has been written in Australia in this century."[5] Although he would be too modest to say so, he himself has shared substantially in this achievement. Once, in an essay about the poetry of his friend Kenneth Slessor he remarked, with characteristic frankness: "I should think that if a nation were on balance worth whooping up, it should be quite possible to whoop it in acceptable poetry."[6] Stewart has done much more than this. His verse dramas *The Fire on the Snow* and *Ned Kelly* are now in an Australian tradition, since they have been part of a course of English studies for tens of thousands of children in this generation, as well as historic radio entertainment for an older one. And if as Robert Graves once said, every poet is finally remembered for a few poems he has written, then Douglas Stewart has achieved immortality in Australian literature with a group of poems including "The Silkworms," "The River," and some of his "Glencoe" ballads—an achievement which most Australian critics have at one time or other conceded.

V *His Part in Australia's Cultural Advancement*

On the other hand it is most significant that Stewart arrived on the Australian literary and artistic scene at a point when its cultural development, despite the incidence of the war years (1939–1945), surged forward with an astonishing velocity. And Stewart became through his *Bulletin* associations, his writing activities, and his personal involvements in his everyday Sydney life, a recognized participant in this movement.

The most exciting advances were in painting and in poetry, with both of which Stewart was particularly and personally involved. But there were other developments also. The steady growth of educational opportunities, despite the Depression years of the early 1930s, saw, by the end of the decade, the emergence of an intellectual-cultural class which, whether as teachers, journalists, writers, or artists, expressed a healthy dissidence. There was a readership for poetry, a listening audience for good radio (to which Stewart powerfully contributed with his verse plays), a body receptive to art and music. It was no accident that the Australian Broadcasting Commission in the 1940s, by increasing the size of its six Australian orchestras, and bringing to Australia many world-famous celebrity artists and conductors, added to this cultural renascence.

Australian painters came into their own during this decade and Stewart, who had married a painter of note (Margaret Coen) and who by his friendship with Norman Lindsay and other artists was an enthusiastic supporter of Australian art, gave impetus to this movement by devoting regular columns in the literary pages of the *Bulletin* to reviews of art shows and informed writing about Australian art. Sidney Nolan, who has since achieved an international reputation, came into his own in this period, as did his fellow Melbourne painters, Arthur Boyd and Albert Tucker. In Sydney, William Dobell, who had just returned after ten years in London, where he had studied at the Slade school, brought new excitement to portrait painting. Russell Drysdale, with the help of ideas drawn from realistic, expressionistic, and even surrealistic sources, followed in various aspects of his painting the experiments which Stewart and some of his fellow writers had essayed in their poetry—approaching the Australian landscape by means of forms and symbolic qualities relating to drought, heat, desert, and the themes of loneliness and melancholy in a hostile environment. In his less serious mood Drysdale depicted some of the "characters" of the Australian outback, often in jocular vein, precisely as Stewart also has done in his poetry from time to time:

> The red cow died and the Hereford bull,
> Two figures more to cancel:
> Dan Corcoran took a bullock's skull
> And wrote on it with a pencil:
>
> "Here I lie on the Birdsville Track
> Driven to death by Scotty Mac."
> Scotty Mac laughed fit to kill,
> Saw it six months later;
> Took another and tried his skill:
> "Here I lie like an old tin can
> Kicked down the Track by droving Dan"—
> Thus drover joked with drover,
> Whether the bullocks laughed as well
> Nobody knows or cares;
> But what they wrote on a bullock's skull
> A bullock could write on theirs.[7]

But most striking of all was the spectacular success of the young poets of the 1940s, marking the high-water level of this tide of cultural creativeness which included not only a resurgence of national aspiration but a new and refreshing awareness of international influences. Tribute must be paid not only to the Sydney *Bulletin,* which under Stewart's inspiring literary editorship gave a forum to many of these poets, but also to the two leading Australian literary journals, *Meanjin* and *Southerly*, which were founded at the beginning of the decade. *Meanjin* (now *Meanjin Quarterly*), especially, set a standard of literary excellence comparable with any literary journal in the world. Soon Judith Wright, 25 in 1940, James McAuley (23), and Douglas Stewart (27), had established themselves as major poets, joining the older poets Kenneth Slessor and R. D. Fitz-Gerald and A. D. Hope (whose output was only sporadic at this stage). Together, as the critic H. P. Heseltine has asserted, they "thrust Australian verse forward with an imperious force unknown since its foundations,"[8] and, what was more important, established the literary climate for the recognition and appreciation of the so many poets of quality who followed, such as Francis Webb, William Hart-Smith, Rosemary Dobson, David Campbell, and ultimately the host of young poets who are, justifiably, the pride of the contemporary Australian literary scene in the 1970s.

CHAPTER 2

Douglas Stewart as Poet

ALTHOUGH Stewart had published ten volumes of poetry between 1936 and 1967 he has simplified the task of the analysis and critical appreciation of his work by editing in 1967 what he regards as a definitive collection of his verses (*Collected Poems 1936–1967*), superseding an earlier anthology, *Selected Poems,* which he had edited and published in 1963. Unless otherwise indicated, therefore, page numbers after quotations which appear in the following pages refer to the *Collected Poems.*

His first volume of poems, *Green Lions* (1936), represented the best of his poetic output to that date, all of it written in New Zealand. He had started writing poetry at the age of fourteen, his original motivation a "compulsory poem" in a school magazine. But he soon became an ardent reader of poetry and recalls[1] that he knew a school textbook, *Smith's Book of Verse,* by heart. He "rapidly" read Shakespeare, Wordsworth, Keats, and Coleridge and other "standard" English poets with great enjoyment. He began contributing his verses to various New Zealand newspapers and journals but especially to the Australian *Bulletin.* "I regularly sent a poem a week to the *Bulletin,*" he wrote once,[2] "which the *Bulletin* with the same unfailing regularity sent back." But he was happy that his early poetry began to be published in a companion journal to the *Bulletin,* the *Australian Women's Mirror,* and this inspired him to continue writing. Although it does not appear in any collection it is interesting to read a poem he wrote at sixteen or seventeen called "Putorino, the Magic Flute," which he "had reconstructed from a couple of translated Maori phrases in some book or other":[3]

> Flute! flute, flute in the emerald gloom,
> you have stolen my soul away,

> and I must go where the red vines bloom
> through the mist of silver and grey
> till the world is lost in the musical leaves
> and the fern roots sink in my heart.
>
> Flute! flute, flute in the emerald gloom,
> I must follow your magical sound
> away from the friends in the firelit room
> till the white mist eddies round
> and the world is lost in the musical leaves
> and the fern roots sink in my heart.

There is even in these early, unpublished lines (probably deriving as much from the early Yeats as from the Maori), the genuine note of poetry, the concern with nature, the affection for color, the grasp of rhythm—elements which have come to so distinguish his later poetry. There is also a note of passion and yearning, which after all should be part of the makeup of any aspiring young poet, and Stewart, writing of his very early poetry, nostalgically recalls that he seemed to have spent his youth "walking about the beautiful green province of Taranaki in a constant state of fury, and a kind of black exaltation..." that he was a "young writer in a country town longing to get out and battle with the world...."[4] Much of his early New Zealand poetry is included in *The White Cry* (1939)—but after that his published collections substantially comprise his Australian writing, though in several books, right up to *Rutherford* and beyond, there are occasional poems with a New Zealand setting.

It would be tempting to deal with his poetry by following the chronological course of his publication of verse, and to talk of his "development" and of the influence of the expanding Australian scene on his poetic experience and sensibility, and so on. Some of this might well be true, but the fact is that much of Stewart's early published work is as "complete," in the full, poetic sense, as that which he has written most recently. It does more justice to his remarkable versatility to deal with his poetry in the various categories into which it can reasonably, if loosely, be shuffled.

James McAuley, a contemporary poet and critic of Stewart,

separating his work as a verse playwright from that as a poet, sees the latter[5] as "roughly classifiable" as narrative poems, poems in a popular quasi-traditional vein with or without fantasy, humorous or satirical poems, meditations and situation pieces, nature studies—chiefly lyrical—and love poems, and observes that these categories "tend to overlap or mingle." Another poet-critic, Vivian Smith, agreeing with these categories, would add another, "the tall-story ballad."[6] However, I think it simpler and quite appropriate to such a study as this (accepting the fact that there is considerable overlapping, and in some cases, poems that are unclassifiable under such headings) to separate Stewart's verse into nature poems, meditations and situation/historical poems, humorous and light verse (including satirical pieces), narrative and ballad poetry, poems which are specifically related to the description of and concern with Australia, and love poems.

I Nature Poetry

Of all his poetry, with its exciting and astonishing variety of subject matter, Stewart's most memorable writing is undoubtedly in his nature poetry, and he himself does not disagree with this view. In his *Seven Rivers*, 1966 (a book of autobiographical essays principally devoted to his great love of fishing), he records his love of the nature poets he likes best—Wordsworth, Clare, Hopkins, Davies, Edmund Blunden—admiring their "essential roughness," wherein they match and reproduce "the roughness of earth or salt water." He admires Tennyson, too, in his nature poetry which, if not having the "freshness of nature" of the other poets, yet reveals "melodious exactitudes of language."[7]

His own poetry, he admits frankly, was "based on nature";[8] that all his poetry started there, that it can be related to his boyhood in the lovely country settings of New Zealand, where his outlook was formed. Environment strongly influences his diction and imagery, even in his earliest poems. Vivian Smith notes that many of his early poems in *Green Lions* "celebrate the southern landscapes of New Zealand and images of ice and snow naturally predominate."[9] There is also cold and frost, and in such an early poem as "Morning in Wellington" one can see the young poet searching for words and images to convey his feeling of bleakness and cold, looking southward to the Antarctic, as it were, even then perhaps projecting his poetic mind to the explorer Scott, and holding, in his imagination, the germinating seeds of his famous radio verse play *The Fire on the Snow.*

Thin stone is in this chill wind from the south,
Thin stone, an essence of those bleak hard hills
That bulk between the town and the cold surf.
Yes, though it gets its coldness from the sea
That snowed with moonlight, icicled with foam
Antarctically glistened all night long,
This current in its planes like panes of glass
That vertically shear between black walls
Is hardened and made sour with those huge hills
As though the sharp spurs gritting through the grass
Exhale their own dank breath into the wind.

Like the lean soul of steel, like spinsters' lips
It has an acid taste, unhumanized.
I think it will be hard for the young birds
And children's lips will blue because of it.
If you had ears like mine you'd hear it now,
Bitter with a thin sound that stone might make
And icy with the far-off ocean breaking,
A cataclysm of surf with frost-toned bells,
Coldly on crag and stone and coldly on cold shells.

(307)

So too with other early poems of his New Zealand period such as "Winter Morning": "Stone cattle are carved on the green, the cows of winter / With no milk firing the shrunken udder" (315), and more remarkably so in "Day and Night with Snow":

... Numb with cold I go
Along a colder and a darker road
To see how tree-ferns like the taste of snow.

(333)

But even in these early nature poems the strength, the almost physical obtruding of his imagery, is remarkable; one could believe he was influenced as much by the Imagist poets of this period, as he may have been by his reading of the metaphysical poets: "The cold, sweet company of moss and stone" ("Shinbone and Moss," 312); "Bronze tempest torrents over from the west / And gongs upon the eastern hill's nude bones" ("Poplar in the Mimi Valley," 316); "The blunt grey statement of New Zealand hills" ("The Growing Strangeness," 318)—and so on. But Stewart ascribes his "violent or pugnacious imagery" of this period to two sources—Roy Campbell and John Cowper Powys, by both of whom he admits he was heavily influenced. Campbell Stewart regarded as a banner for the colonial poets of the time: "he had gone over and conquered England and we thought we might go and do likewise." From Campbell too he confesses he picked up "that pernicious habit of using nouns as verbs."[10]

But this starkness, this brooding quality in his contemplation of nature (very much due to his obsession with the work of Cowper Powys, he admits) disappeared almost magically when he came to Australia and began writing the long and glorious succession of nature poems for which he is now so distinguished and in which has emerged the lyric quality generally absent in the poems of his New Zealand period. This is not to say that an intensity of observation, a quality of deep, philosophical introspection does not still remain in these earlier poems. One is reminded of "The Green Centipede" (a poem from his *Sun Orchids,* 1952, collection, which contains some of his most characteristic nature pieces):

Whatever lies under a stone
Lies under the stone of the world:
That day of the yellow flowers
When out of moss and shale
The cassia bushes unfurled
Their pale soft yellow stars
And lit the whole universe,
Out from the same deep source
Like some green shingly rill
From the grey stone dislodged

> The big green centipede ran
> Rippling down from the hill:
> And fringed with silvery light,
> So beautiful, not to be touched,
> In its green grace had power
> —Down where all rivers meet
> Deep under stony ground—
> To make the most gentle flower
> Burn, burn in the hand.
>
> (159)

Stewart has explained to me[11] that at the time he wrote this poem he was quite consciously interested in exploring the duality of the universe, good and evil, beauty and ugliness, God and the Devil, and so on—and on a mountainside near the home of his friend Norman Lindsay, at Springwood near Sydney, he found a field of magnificent yellow flowers. Walking among them he kicked over a stone and disturbed this "big green centipede." Suddenly he realized that the flower and the centipede must have come from the same creative force—and that this force, whatever it was, so gentle in the flower was strong enough to burn in the hand, like a centipede.

Stewart's fellow poet R. D. FitzGerald[12] has commented on Stewart's predilection toward a nature poet's mysticism—that his short nature pieces taken separately seem to be exquisite miniatures drawn from nature, but considered together constitute the framework of a philosophy of mysticism. Stewart takes his small birds, animals, insects, and flowers, embodies them imaginatively in the smallest possible compass, compresses them, so to speak, into an instant of their being so that we have the illusion of a momentary reality. Thus "Grasshopper":

> And then the red stone hopped
> Where all the stones were red
> And it had legs like a frog
> And a big strange insect's head.
> Oh where's the green world gone
> When even the grasshopper turns
> To a kind of dragon of the sun
> In a land of hopping stones?
>
> (127)

thus "Goldfish"

> They nibble at the feet of wasps,
> They prowl for algae in the lilies
> Or standing on their heads deep down
> Display a flash of silver bellies.
>
> (58)

thus "Waterlily"

> All images and fancies coalesce and cancel
> In mystery at last; it is an angel,
> And moves its yellow wings above the water.
>
> (59)

It would seem in these, and so many of his other short nature lyrics, that Stewart is contriving, in form as well as in subject matter, to make each poem no larger than the subject itself, so that as a small part of the objective universe it both embodies and is embodied in an underlying reality. It is a concept of achieving identity with some aspect of nature and at the same time of reaching toward identity with what may lie beyond nature. FitzGerald also remarks that this is a concept:

related to Wordsworth's pantheism—and Stewart greatly admires Wordsworth, though more, I fancy, for his detail than for his philosophy—but it differs from Wordsworth in that Stewart has little of Wordsworth's monism in his outlook. He may be prepared to recognize an ultimate Unity, but he has not Wordsworth's obsession with a majestic universal immanence in Nature. On the contrary, he makes a plurality of parts each represent the whole and absorb the whole, rather than have all the parts absorbed into one pervading unity. The ultimate Unity he leaves strictly alone, presumably because it is unknowable. Instead, he concerns himself with the intermediate aspects in which his own identity too might be recognizable. . . .[13]

Although throughout Stewart's poetry one detects some change in his idiom, his philosophy, his attitude, even his imagery, there remains throughout his nature poetry the constant of a simple, lyrical quality. It is hard to believe that in his magical capacity to use words not only economically, but to

triumphant and enduring poetic effect, he has not been influenced by Edward Thomas ("Out of us all / That make rhymes /
will you choose / sometimes").[14] A Stewart poem written in
recent years like "Wasp":

> Well wasp what's
> To do about you
> Battering at the windscreen
> You can't get through?
>
> World's all wrong,
> Air itself in treason
> Suddenly turns solid
> And shuts you in prison.
>
> And still through the wall wasp
> The long green paddocks sweeten
> With trigger-flower and daisy
> And gold billy-button;
>
> But up wasp down wasp
> Climb wasp and fall,
> Can't beat your way
> Through the clear strange wall.
>
> Out and away then
> When the car stops;
> World's come right again
> And happy goes wasp.
>
>   (29)

enraptures no more and no less than his almost perfect lyric
"Stream and Shadows" from his *The White Cry* (1939) collection:

> Still in the rivery shadows,
> Her calm is a white flowing
> Her silence is a song
> Of darkened silver, knowing
>
> No word but that of water
> No life that stream's cool grace,

By silver sands, dark hollows,
And softly through the grass

To what black wave will break
In foam of stars and flutes,
Flowing in white and singing
Dark silver as she floats.

(296)

Both these lyrics afford an interesting example of Stewart's cavalier attitude to the conventions of rhyme: "sweeten" / "button," "stops" / "wasp," "grace" / "grass"—examples can be multiplied throughout his poetry. In one of his more serious poems he has even rhymed "Icarus" with "licorice." He just as blandly used unexpected rhymes for a set and successful purpose, as in "A Country Song": "Schute, Bell, Badgery, Lumby / How's your dad and how'd your mum be?" (66). It is a part of his approach to poetry whereby he is constantly extending his use of colloquialism, using vigorous rhythms and refrains, employing slang words and phrases if its suits his purpose in order to create what James McAuley has described as "a sort of literary populism."[15] Admittedly "popular" poetry sometimes succumbs to the Philistine notion that there is a fit place for everything. But if there is such a thing as a poetry of public satisfaction for common understanding and celebration, a poetry to be linked and *used* again and again, then Stewart has achieved this. Certainly it explains why he is one of the most widely read, if not *the* most widely read of contemporary Australian poets.

The fact is that what are widely held to be Stewart's best-known poems are his pieces, incapable of having nonexistent subtleties read into them, that tell of foxes, frogs, kookaburras, finches, bees, flying ants, even cicadas where he has modeled an unforgettable lyric on the traditional salute to spring:

Summer is icumen in,
Loud sing cicada!
Bulljo nippeth, black snake slippeth
Sun biteth harder.

Treetops ring with peals of light
(Merry sing Greengrocer!)
Red bark cracketh, blue smoke tracketh,
Bushfire stealeth closer.
Sing cicada!

("Cicada Song," 121)

There is, of course, a perfectly sound reason for this choice
of subject: Stewart's scrupulous observation of the minutiae of
creatures and things, rendered in a tone tenderly elegiac, or
matter-of-fact or joyously humorous. As any Australian who
frequents the bush and outback of his country well knows,
the most frolicsome and rowdy of birds is the magpie—whose
antics Stewart has caught magnificently and set in his poetic
amber in "Sunshower":

If he had sung a white song for every white feather
That wicked old magpie had sinned for every black
But clear he carolled on the gum-tree behind the shack
For it was a mad season of black-and-white weather
When sunshowers swept the mountains in dazzling waves
And shadow and shine seemed mixed in one tower of joy!
And loud he sang, then like some larrikin boy
Magpie and sunshower, splashing on the wet bright leaves,
Tobogganed down the old green tree together.

(161)

There is this same facility in his delightful evocation of the
antics of another playful Australian bird, the gang-gang. Here
again is the microscopic view of a part of the world of nature,
an almost deliberate zoning of sensibility within these limits, a
controlled flow of feeling which nevertheless allows a full focus
on the behavior and antics of the birds themselves. In this poem,
as in a number of other nature poems, Stewart uses the device
of anthropomorphism only to the extent needed for us to estab-
lish kinship with his birds (or flowers, or insects), without
affecting the reality of the situation.

Some sleep like flowers big and soft and dark,
Some lift their crests up in a crimson ruffle

And light the leaves of that old candlebark
Or make it dance as they bob heads and shuffle.

Some sharpen their great beaks on hard dead wood
And nip the twigs off in a leafy rain,
Some spread their wings and flare in fighting mood
That's all pretence, then fall to sleep again.

Some preen each other, some to show their skill
Hang upside down like bats from the high branches
While drowsy lovers nibble bill to bill
With horny kisses and with sidelong glances.
                    ("A Flock of Gang-Gangs," 75)

One is moved to make the incidental observation that if the
first test of a poet is how nearly the language he uses belongs
to himself and his particular time, place, circumstances, how
little it springs from imitations of others, then from such a
passage as this, and so many others—particularly where Stewart describes Australian birds and animals—there is always the
right response.

Many Australian poets, predecessors as well as contemporaries of Stewart, have specialized in nature poetry, have sung,
as it were, the bush and its denizens: some, like Judith Wright,
Australia's foremost lyric poet, have subordinated the actual
subject matter of the poetry to poetic technique (as indeed
Shaw Neilson did long before Judith Wright). Others, like
Henry Kendall, in a previous century used Australian sights,
sounds, birds, and beasts to conjure up a nostalgic, romantic
re-creation of an England from which they were in exile. Others
yet again, like David Campbell, Stewart's friend and contemporary, have created a sort of Australian pastoral tradition
by adapting classic forms of poetry to the topics and themes
of nature. All these manifestations have been necessary and important phases in the ecology of Australian poetry.[16]

Stewart, however, differs from almost every Australian who
has written or writes nature poetry. He is seldom emotional in
his approach, much more inclined to be clinically observant,
to record and report with every lyrical artifice he considers
appropriate. Within these limits he is often droll, certainly drier

in tone, sometimes even inclined to moralize. Sometimes he will even create a world of fantasy within the theme or subject of his nature poem, as in his conceit of a waterlily as an angel:

> Look, look, there is an angel in the fishpond,
> It wakes its yellow wings above the water. . . .
> ("Waterlily," 59)

or of the colorful desert flowers, Christmas bells, as:

> . . . wild children
> Running in their straight frocks
> Of boldest orange and vermilion
> All day in the sandstone rocks;
> ("Christmas Bells," 110)

Yet at no time, as Vivian Smith observes, does Stewart entertain such an image or fantasy for any other reason than its poetic usefulness: "the poetic strength of this fantasy world resides in the fact that the author himself does not fully believe in it."[17] In other words, as a nature poet Stewart is wholly aesthetic.

II *Meditative Poetry*

Stewart's most recent writing has undoubtedly concentrated on meditative themes and pieces of a situational or historical nature. But even though he is known to most readers primarily as a nature and lyric poet, he has always had a penchant for philosophizing in verse; the difference is that he has in his later poetry become more dispassionate and ironic. As early as his *Green Lions* (1956) collection Stewart had a quite remarkable facility (for a young poet) to let his mind brood on ordinary experiences, using them to summon ghosts from the past, or, with metaphysical imagery, as a probe for something buried deeper in men's consciousnesses. Snow on the countryside evoked the strangest thoughts of "troubling and pianoing desire"; as he warily walked through the white stillness he realized that "one might taste the pale-green wine of madness / Too deeply drinking at this faery chalice." Further, amid the dank bush,

Snow lines the vines with silver, veins the leaves
And soaks the dark-green sponges of the moss;
Snow sprawls like fungus on the rotting logs
And drags the living earthwards like a cross.
("Day and Night with Snow," 332)

There is remarkable sensibility in these reactions. We see it too in another poem of the same period, "The Winter-Crazed," where the New Zealand countryside, besieged by winter, evokes the most bizarre fantasies in his mind, so that "hedge is beast and hills like tigers purr / And stones like old men cough or moan like shells." The poet's humanity is aroused; he compassionately turns his thoughts to the humdrum lives of those around him:

Only the flickerlands of books or talkies
More vivid shadows, give us sense of living;
Our eyes prefer the easier illusion
To morning's mistiness and day's confusion.
There in the black-and-white we do our loving,
Murder and laugh and cry with great content
Assured of life since living we are leaving.
(320)

It is striking how even as a young poet Stewart was capable of moments of intense understanding. In "Died in Harness" (314), a short poem in which tragic irony and the inevitability of death jostle together, the last line expresses a moment of superb vision:

At his desk, with its litter of papers, the old man died:
And it seemed in the morning
With its frolic of children in rhythms of blue and gold,
The rattle of dishes, the bustle of men into offices,
The rustle of morning papers,
A great bell tolled
Grow old ... grow old ... we all grow old ...
The scratch of a million pens, the clatter of typists, hushed:

And in all the world that moment no man was bought or sold.
(314)

Chronologically there follows a string of poems of this type. "Elegy for an Airman," written in memory of a boyhood friend killed in action with the R.A.F. in 1939, concludes with one of Stewart's most brilliant and emotional statements:

> . . . caught in its day your silver statement of laughter
> Is a fountain they cannot bury under the clay.
> O my friend, your life goes echoing on through time
> As the thrush still rings in the mind when the willows darken.
>
> (275)

"The River" (247), written some years later, has evoked the genuine admiration of Stewart's fellow poets; R. D. FitzGerald once wrote of it that "it stands so high that it will always come to mind when one is considering Douglas Stewart at his best."[18] It is one of the few biographical poems he has written, recalling his New Zealand boyhood and the spiritual influences of the rugged Mt. Egmont country and its rushing streams upon his intellectual development. Nancy Keesing in her study of Stewart considers that this poem was "of pivotal importance in his development as a poet" and in it "for the first time his high imagination blends with rich resources of language."[19]

Certainly Stewart uses sustained imagery throughout the poem with confidence and power. The river (as the river of life) is pure and crystal clear at its source where the Egmont snows have melted, the home of the wild duck returned from hibernation to her spring nesting place, "bound to that place by what mysterious love." So Stewart himself is bound, all his life:

> Passion and disaster, knowledge of love and hate,
> Battle of mind and body against the world
> Where the rivers of men and traffic roared and swirled,
> The lonely rage of the spirit wrestling with fate:
> So much went into the making of a man.
> But always under the struggle, oh deep below,
> The grey stones stood, and one clear river ran
> And into the sea of a life brought down the snow.

and, like the wild duck, symbol of his own poetic soul, he will inevitably return as he declares in his passionately beautiful final statement to his "one clear river"

At the end of life illusion falls away,
When the city falls, oh then in that last day, river,
I shall come back to you as a man to his lover,
As the bird comes back when her wild blood sets the day
And the first leaf breaks on the willow. Symbol or truth.
Let the day disclose! But a man's what his spirit knows;
And what I have known for truth, now as in youth,
Is one clear river, coming down cold from the snows.

(247)

But Stewart was to reach new poetic heights in the discursive mode with "Rutherford" (96), the title poem of his 1962 collection. As in "The River," he uses an eight-line stanza with a long-striding rhythm, though rhyming abab, cdcd rather than abba, cdcd. But the effect of breadth and room for a theme's gradual poetic development is admirably sustained. This long poem of thirty-six stanzas has been effectively described by James McAuley as "a meditation in the form a personality-revealing monologue";[20] its general theme, handled with finesse and mastery, is the nature of responsibility and power; its particular theme, the picture of a great physicist at the pinnacle of his career and on the verge of even more epoch-making discoveries:

It was the most fascinating thing in the world
And out of it too, like watching some new star:
To go in there and watch the atom unfold
Its innermost secrets, right to the very core
Where star within star the racing electrons whirled
Circling that radiant centre, the white-hot nucleus,
—Held in your hands, almost, huge as you were,
Pierced by your thought like a neutron. It was miraculous

How out of steel and glass, coiled wire and lead,
The common stuff of the earth (what else could you use?),
Mere human powers could have conceived and made
These infinitely delicate instruments to pierce
Clean through matter to its end. . . .

(96)

There is a subtle intermingling of themes: the scientist whose researches are concerned for the good of mankind; the inevitable

progress of knowledge and its effects on the future of the human
race; Rutherford's recurring obsession with the symbol of the
wheel; a wheel which "moved somewhere far away in the dark";
the waterwheel which his father, a wheelwright, had made when
he (Rutherford) was a youth:

> That waterwheel of his father's lifted up
> Water and sunlight in its wooden hands
> Where the weed grew like hair, then let them drop
> Back to the stream that sang on over the sands. . . .
>
> (97)

and eventually the galactic wheel of the universe

> The universe turned and moved above him so vast
> Full of black space, the huge wheel slowly spinning,
>
> (99)

It is the interweaving of these themes that give structural power
and coherence to the poem, magnificently sustained from its
beginning when Rutherford, in his study at Cambridge, ponders
the riddle of piercing the nucleus of the atom. We see his doubts
and uneasiness about the disastrous results that might occur
("you could pay dearly / For probing too deeply into that dark
resistance / Where light lay   coiled like stone. . . ."); his yearn-
ings for the simple life of a New Zealand farmer "under
snowy Egmont"; his realization, however, that he must go on—
"a man alive must show what he can do"; his vision of the
future:

> With what it had dreamed of: not just his own ambition
> But all mankind's, Lord knows what power beside,
> Came here to some great moment of fruition
> And into the future cast its glittering seed.
> So now in God's name, thinking of nuclear fission
> And looking out of the window into the dark
> Where lay the whole teeming world that man had made,
> London, Paris, Berlin, Moscow, New York. . . .
>
> (103)

Finally, Stewart, with appropriate images of brightness ("crystal, "radiant," "clear morning," "sun") has Rutherford reconciled to the work that must be done:

> And yet as he looked at the sky so dark with warning
> Vast over earth and its towers, the night heaved over
> Close and familiar as a waterwheel turning
> And shed its stars like drops of crystal water
> And radiant over the world lay the clear morning.
> Men moved in darkness truly, but also in the sun
> And on that huge bright wheel that turned for ever
> He left his thought, for there was work to be done.
>
> (105)

It is in the last line of the poem that the full measure of Stewart's achievement is apparent—that he has equated the personality of Rutherford (as revealed through a type of interior monologue) with his awareness of and dedication toward his responsibilities as a great scientist.

Stewart in some of his recent meditative studies has adopted a slightly ironical stance; indeed there is an overlapping with poems of this type which one could more justifiably classify as humorous verse. "Fence" (62) is a good example of this: it is equally an example of Stewart's desire to use poetry "to sing the universe into shape"[21] by taking what appears to be a most prosaic subject and turning it into poetry. "Fence must be looked at; fence is too much neglected; / Most ancient indeed is fence..." begins the poet disarmingly, and then develops his theme round the affairs of a typical, suburban family named Hogan:

> But fence is earthwork, *defensa*; connected no doubt
> With *fossa*, a moat; straight from the verb to defend;
> Therefore ward off, repel, stand guard on the moat;
> None climbs this fence but cat or Hogan's friend.
> Fence is of spears and brambles; fence is defiance
> To sabre-toothed tigers, to all the world in the end,
> And there behind it the Hogans stand like lions.

A similar poetic technique, half waggish, half serious but developing verities that are sociologically appropriate to modern man's lifestyle can be discerned in Stewart's poem "Horse" (64). Horse, looking over the fence, sees "a world too fine for words," and is, in his equine introspection, unmoved until

> ... down the sunny road
> Flashing like proud relations
> To far bright destinations
> The cars come silent-hooved
> Then indeed he is moved:
> Like swans in water they wander
> All through his dim brain's wonder.
> The world's magnificence
> Over the high board fence
> Passes all eloquence. ...

No discussion of Stewart's meditative verse could be concluded without reference to "The Silkworms" (49). It is a masterpiece which must be quoted in full not only to illustrate the sophistication of poetic technique Stewart has reached, with its haunting use of half-rhymes and rhyming overtones (or short rhymes), but also to demonstrate the imaginative insight of his approach. He sees the silkworm, correctly, as spinning in a tradition that is ancient and timeless; indeed his power to evoke the sense of agelessness is especially notable—"ancestral voices"; "forbidden, forbidden"; (we think immediately of the "Forbidden City"); "little dragon." And finally, there is the ineffable beauty of the last stanza.

> All their lives in a box! What generations,
> What centuries of masters, not meaning to be cruel
> But needing their labour, taught these creatures such patience
> That now though sunlight strikes on the eye's dark jewel
> Or moonlight breathes on the wing they do not stir
> But like the ghosts of moths crouch silent there.

> Look it's a child's toy! There is no lid even,
> They can climb, they can fly, and the whole world's their tree;
> But hush, they say in themselves, we are in prison.
> There is no word to tell them that they are free,
> And they are not; ancestral voices bind them
> In dream too deep for wind or word to find them.

Even in the young, each like a little dragon
Ramping and green upon his mulberry leaf,
So full of life, it seems, the voice has spoken:
They hide where there is food, where they are safe,
And the voice whispers, "Spin the cocoon,
Sleep, sleep, you shall be wrapped in me soon."

Now is their hour, when they wake from that long swoon;
Their pale curved wings are marked in a pattern of leaves,
Shadowy for trees, white for the dance of the moon;
And when on summer nights the buddleia gives
Its nectar like lilac wine for insects mating
They drink its fragrance and shiver, impatient with waiting,

They stir, they think they will go. Then they remember
It was forbidden, forbidden, ever to go out;
The Hands are on guard outside like claps of thunder,
The ancestral voice says Don't, and they do not.
Still the night calls them to unimaginable bliss
But there is terror around them, the vast, the abyss,

And here is the tribe that they know, in their known place,
They are gentle and kind together, they are safe for ever,
And all shall be answered at last when they embrace.
White moth moves closer to moth, lover to lover.
There is that pang of joy on the edge of dying—
Their soft wings whirr, they dream that they are flying.

III   Narrative and Ballad Poetry

Douglas Stewart has explained[22] that in his 1944 collection
of poems, The Dosser in Springtime, he began experimenting
with ballad forms partly because he liked the "dance of the
rhythm," partly because he was thinking of poetry in terms of a
narration—"not an exploration of the author's own state of mind,
but though you might still have a personal reason for writing it,
a story about some real or imagined incident, a dramatization."
Some of his experimentation produced poetry that was, at best,
uneven—often trite:

> Somebody stole our mountain,
> The valley people cried;

Widgetty Creek has vanished,
Bindo Creek has dried.
The sparrowhawk searching the heavens
For its nest in the ironbark
Screams in a burning nowhere
From empty dawn to dark.
("The Stolen Mountain," 258)

On the other hand in poems like "Old Iron" (231), "Ball and Chain" (237), and especially "Child and Lion" (250), Stewart showed that he was achieving a blend of narrative colloquialism, a strong control of rhythm, and more and more a blending of symbolism and allegory:

I watch that lion and the whole world reels,
Said the woman to the pigeons in the park;
God alone knows what a mother's heart feels
When she watches her daughter as she laughs and kicks her heels,
Riding on the back of the lion.

There was moss on his mane and his flanks were stone,
Said the woman to the pigeons in the park;
And he stretched out his limbs with a kind of rocky groan,
And the stone lion walked and my daughter was gone,
Riding on the back of the lion.

(250)

At any rate these poems made up the impetus carrying him forward to his most ambitious and successful book of poems, *Glencoe* (1947), which was a series of ballads in varying forms, of the Highland tragedy of 1692, when the Campbells attempted to massacre an entire clan of MacDonalds. Several years before writing these ballads Stewart had visited the actual scene of the massacre during a trip through Scotland; he had some personal interest in this seemingly remote theme for it was to his own ancestors, the Stewarts of Appin, that the survivors of the MacDonalds fled for refuge.

There is a structural simplicity in the planning of the cycle, which begins with a ballad set in an Edinburg alehouse some months after the event; moves back in a flashback technique to the clannish enmities and politics which led to the massacre;

covers the massacre itself and the aftermath, and then reverts to the alehouse scene, and to a highland soldier, "bottle-nosed Jock," who thus is, as it were, the link in the sequence.

> "The first the day," says bottle-nosed Jock,
> And down he sinks his toddy;
> "If ye'll pay for my grog till the crack o' dawn
> I'll drink wi' ony body."
>
> (197)

Stewart shows a remarkable mastery of ballad styles and rhythms throughout the cycle, R. D. FitzGerald has remarked that "*Glencoe* might almost seem to have been written under direct inspiration from one of Stewart's own Scottish ancestors."[23] The complicated series of events which led to the massacre are set out simply and confidently so that comprehension is never strained and the magic note of the authentic ballad is never lost. Stewart finds a suitable form for each event in the story. The machinations of the Earl of Breadalbane, a leader of the clan Campbell, are rendered in a long flowing line which gives continuity and verisimilitude to the story of the plotting:

Breadalbane's eyes are black as the peat, narrow and darkly
  glowing:
"And when the MacDonalds came down frae the Isles would all of
  their deeds bear showing?
. . . ."

(203)

The dramatic, supernatural quality of the Scottish ballad is used with feeling and force, to give background to the march of events:

> "I fear the night of snow and wind
>   (*Lord, man, you're dead*)
> The snowflakes beat the pony blind,
> But most I fear the journey's end
> For never yet was the English king
> A chief o' Scotland's friend."
>
> (205)

A swift, racing note—the traditional galloping rhythm—denotes the increasing tempo toward an approaching climax:

> The Earl of Breadalbane paces the room
> Darkens his face with the cloud of doom:
> "The king must agree but we'll manage him,"
> Says the black Earl of Breadalbane.
>
> (209)

Again the long-lined ballad form is used to lead into the massacre:

> "And who do I love if I love not me, now half of the night is
>   gone?"
> Glenlyon strides in MacIan's hall and screams to his men, "Fall
>   on!"
>
> (218)

complemented by the shorter-lined form with the telling use of repetition:

> "Dinna ye see the blazin' torch,
> Dinna ye smell the smoke,
> Dinna ye hear the yells o' death
> Frae the huts o' your tenant folk?
> . . . ."
>
> (219)

But Stewart reaches the peak of his poetic talent in a stark and moving account of the aftermath, seen from a distance of time, full of pity and compassion, the most simple yet telling poetry imaginable, as only genuine ballad-form could convey it:

> Sigh, wind in the pine;
> River, weep as you flow;
> Terrible things were done
> Long, long ago.
>
> In daylight golden and mild
> After the night of Glencoe
> They found the hand of a child
> Lying upon the snow.

> Lopped by the sword to the ground
> Or torn by wolf or fox,
> That was the snowdrop they found
> Among the granite rocks.
>
> Oh, life is fierce and wild
> And the heart of the earth is stone,
> And the hand of a murdered child
> Will not bear thinking on.
>
> Sigh, wind in the pine,
> Cover it over with snow;
> But terrible things were done
> Long, long ago.
>
> (220)

It is in this penultimate sequence ("bottle-nosed Jock" completes the cycle back in the alehouse) that we can appreciate the sincerity of Stewart's later statement that "the theme is not really remote . . . it is a protest against barbarity, cruelty and violence in any age."[24]

Stewart followed his Glencoe poems with a series called "Worsley Enchanted" (175), based on the explorer Sir Ernest Shackleton's voyage to the Antarctic in 1914. Commander Worsley was the captain of Shackleton's ship, the *Endurance*. Stewart's narrative in various stanza and metrical forms, and with his own commentary introducing each poem in the sequence, describes the events and experiences of Shackleton's men after their ship was wrecked in the pack-ice, when having drifted for six months on an ice-floe, they were able then to make their way in the ship's boats to Elephant Island, an uninhabited rock in the far south. Stewart's ostensible aim, in the poems, is to convey the strangeness of the Antarctic world as it appeared to Worsley, a plain and unsophisticated seaman. This he does, both by word pictures, as in Worsley's meditations on the strange sight of nine Emperor penguins which suddenly appeared from a crack in the ice on the day the *Endurance* was wrecked:

> Oh, there was broken wood,
> There were weeds of iron and rope

The log that was bigger than a tree
Crashed on the frozen sea
And the tall dark penguins stood
And stared at the ice without hope,
Said the nine Emperor penguins.

And these were a race of birds
Majestic, beyond belief;
There where the gold mist hung
They spoke in a foreign tongue,
Loud, sharp, excited words,
They rocked and shook with grief,
Said the nine Emperor penguins.
(177)

and by dramatically descriptive verse as in Shackleton's agony at finding and losing the land of South Georgia:

There on the ledge there is rock, there are tussocks growing,
There are runnels of water flowing, it is land, it is life,
It is victory white and tremendous; and a breath is blowing
Of hurricane coming; and we cannot land in that surf.
Turn her to sea, said Shackleton staring in horror,
Where is the land? There is only shadow and spray
And the howl of the gale and the seething of broken water—
They could not do it, they could not take it away.
(186)

As Stewart has explained,[25] this sequence of poems is, by implication, a comment on the strangeness of all human experience, the mystery of our existence. But his obsession with Antarctic exploration, in the middle period of his writing, also carried the implication that he saw in the explorer (as he did later in the scientist) the figure who deserved to be commemorated in his poetry as one who quested truth and the enlargement of the human mind.

In other narrative poems Stewart has delighted in taking imaginary historical encounters and using them not only to carry a note of philosophic enquiry but also to engage his considerable flair for dialogue in verse, perfected by his previous playwriting.

Thus in "Terra Australis" (168) he imagines a meeting some-where in the Pacific between Captain Quiros, an idealist who thought he had discovered a paradise of the South when he landed in the New Hebrides Islands in 1606, and one William Lane, a radical Australian visionary who left Australia in 1893 with a small band of hopeful followers, to found a utopian New Australia in Paraguay. The poetry is strong, bold, and chal-lenging; the dialogue is hammered out in commanding accents:

> "What ship?" "The *Royal Tar!*" "And whither bent?"
> "I seek the new Australia." "I, too, stranger;
> Terra Australis, the great continent
> That I have sought three centuries and longer;
>
> "And westward still it lies, God knows how far,
> Like a great golden cloud, unknown, untouched,
> Where men shall walk at last like spirits of fire
> No more by oppression chained, by sin besmirched."
>
> "Westward there lies a desert where the crow
> Feeds upon poor men's hearts and picks their eyes;
> Eastward we flee from all that wrath and woe
> And Paraguay shall yet be Paradise."
>
> "Eastward," said Quiros, as *San Pedro* rolled,
> High-pooped and round in the belly like a barrel,
> "Men tear each other's entrails out for gold;
> And even here I find that men will quarrel."

Similarly in his most recent collection is "Mungo Park" (39), an imaginative account of a meeting which actually took place between Park and Sir Walter Scott in the countryside of Scot-land. Stewart's conclusion, conveyed through their parting words, is an interesting reflection of his own philosophy as a poet whose talent has matured both in versatility and technique:

> "Each to his trade, and mine's to walk, Sir Walter;
> Yet in the countries never seen by men
> Who's paid the greater price, who's gone the further,
> I with my travels, you with your midnight pen?

My road lies far; yet it could be, my friend,
In mile and mile we go or book and book
We take the same strange journey in the end.
What can we do but wish each other luck?"

Then up the misty hill they rode together.
"I dinna trust your luck," Sir Walter said
When Mungo's horse lost footing in the heather.
But Mungo laughed and rode on straight ahead.
"We'll smile at that," he said, "when I get back,"
And parted so, as it turned out for ever,
Sir Walter to his candle and his book
And Mungo to the light on his blue river.

IV *Humorous, Satirical and Light Verse*

This classification, chosen for the sake of expediency, is misleading, because very little of Stewart's published poetry deserves to be classified directly as "humorous." Rather it is that elements of humor, wit, gentle irony, and quiet satire appear frequently in his poetry and provide, as James McAuley so aptly put it, "sunlight and salt."[26] Stewart describes this as "trying to be yourself. If you have a naturally humorous outlook or humorous turn of speech . . . it should come out in your verse, I don't see why you can't laugh in serious poetry." He regards the "breakthrough" from the "seriousness and agony and Roy Campbell swashbuckling" of his earlier poetry, as occurring in a poem called "The Bishop" (262), which was first published in his 1946 collection *The Dosser in Springtime*—and which enabled him then to write "more naturally and humorously about things."[27]

"The Bishop" is a playful meditation about a statue in a Sydney park and Stewart's drollery is exemplified in his relating of the stiff immobility of the bishop, with his "eyes as cold as a Gorgon's," to the high life and low life of the city teeming about him:

The rich and the poor, the strong and the weak, the priest and
    sinner and sot,
Whether they like it or whether they don't the bishop blesses the
    lot.

. . . . .
I mightn't have liked the bishop alive but I certainly like him
    dead,
The good old man in his suit of bronze with the pigeon on top of
    his head;

Solid in space, secure in time, defiant he takes his stand,
The whole of life goes blessed on its way beneath the sun of his
    hand.

                                                               (263)

Now while Stewart is quite capable of writing splendid light
verse—and indeed Vivian Smith counts him as "undoubtedly
the most distinguished writer of light verse that Australia has
produced,"[28] and cites such poems as "Professor Piccard" (45),
"Leopard Skin" (61), and "Familiars" (77) in support of his
contention—the true measure of Stewart's achievement in this
respect is his capacity, unique among his contemporaries, to
inject humor into serious poetry, without in any way reducing
the poetic quality of his work. Stewart is an innovator among
Australian poets in this regard and it is this ability which gives
a characteristic and memorable note to some of his verse.

"Reflections at a Parking Meter" (15) is an excellent example
of this technique. The poet, troubled by the carnage wrought
by the motor car, "Has paused in protest by a parking meter /
And switched his engine off to make this statement." He knows
that men change: that man "had his propensity / For taking on
the force if not appearance / Of anything he rode. . . ." But
with the motor car it is worst of all:

    For once we had the car from the inventor,
    The horseless carriage, then the swift tin lizzie,
    Man made it, we could see, his only mentor.
    There was no harm at first, the pace was easy,
    The man and car joined calmly like a centaur;
    But soon, as we know well, the roads went crazy.

    Some saw the true position quite reversed;
    The car, they said, was just a starter button
    That loosed man's own fierce passions at their worst;
    Fired with the chance it gave he stamped his foot on

His own accelerator in a burst
That knocked his fellows down like so much mutton.

. . . . .

To go go go became his natural function:
So cars met cars, there was no real driver,
And crashed on curves and bumped at each road junction;
Cars cursed at cars and knocked each other over,
Cars pushed through city crowds without compunction.
The wonder is that there was one survivor.

What Stewart moves us to reflect upon in such a poem as this
(and others such as "One Yard of Earth" (5) and "Farewell to
Jindabyne" (19) he has written in recent years) is that the com-
plexity and arrogance of the technological civilization which
confuses and threatens the literary values with which most
serious readers of poetry have grown up, calls for a special
kind of detailed understanding and critical stamina. It is something to do also with undramatic rational patience and hard,
constructive thinking, the sort of response required for the social
and political challenges of a world of overpopulation, pollution,
and violence—the world with which Stewart, in such poems as
these, clearly hopes that poetry will explicitly connect. As he
has put it quite clearly in his critical writing, "I think what has
chiefly been going on in Australian poetry in this century is a
re-discovery and re-assessment of the whole Australian environment. . . . Perhaps, except when writers have retreated into the
ivory tower the same thing can be said about the poetry of any
country at any period. . . . But I think that in a new country
it is something that happens with particular urgency."[29]
Normally Stewart's use of irony is gentle and tolerant: he
is not a crusader; he prefers to view the follies and foibles of
mankind with an observant and an unjaundiced eye. Yet, on
the occasion of the prosecution of the publishers of *Lady Chat-
terley's Lover* in England, Stewart, a lifelong opponent of censorship in any form, used his humor like a rapier to write a
poetic indictment of the prudery which had launched this liti-
gation; though at the same time, with a double irony, he ques-
tions the aesthetic value of the four-letter words over which
the battle was fought. His "Four-Letter Words"—". . . Rejoice,

all souls, I sing four-letter words..." (19)—has thus become one of his best-known poems.

There was a word they'd never dreamed of uttering,
Its letters reached the mystic total four.
Could they refrain when freedom's lamp was guttering
And one small breath would blow it bright once more?
While judges quailed and pressmen blessed their luck
Each one in turn pronounced the brave word ——.

They said it once they said it twice and thrice,
They jumped for joy, they made the welkin ring,
It sounded queer, it sounded rather nice;
And, what was the extraordinary thing,
In town or village, bathroom, church or bed,
All over England not a soul dropped dead.

And round the world the glorious news was rung
For though in swamps like Eire or Australia
Some fogs of ancient prejudice still clung,
The law proclaimed in pomp and full regalia
That books could now be printed, poems sung
In words direct and down to earth as dung.

(21)

The gift of sustaining effortless wit and whimsy in his poetry comes naturally to Stewart; it is one thing to be able to write in this way in prose (which of course Stewart is able to do), but another to carry it off in poetry without tumbling over the ever-present precipice, once the difficult journey is begun, into the abyss of trite facetiousness or vulgarity. But Stewart keeps his foothold cleverly, and while this is due in part to his essentially comic vision of the universe and its people it is also a matter of conscious striving in his writing. As Nancy Keesing has noted:

Even apparently impromptu humour is frequently the result of long writing, revision and hard work, the more so, perhaps, because humour *does* come easily to Stewart in dazzling conversation and rapid repartee; in the intensely funny notes he dashes off where another man would content himself with prosy memoranda; in puns;

in the odd slants and juxtapositions that make many of his poems memorable.[30]

It is the wide-ranging scope of his poetic humor that is perhaps most remarkable of all in this aspect of his writing; and yet it remains Stewart's most satisfying way of commenting on life and living. In "Two Englishmen" (13) two lonely camel-riders in the desert are embarrassed, with proper British reserve, at the prospect of greeting strangers:

> And so passed by, erect, superb, absurd,
> Across the desert sands without a word.

So Stewart encapsulates in a few lines centuries of the mores and lifestyle of the typical upperclass Englishman. In "Bill Posters" (234) he wilfully but wittily maintains his atrociously funny pun till the bitter end—"Bill Posters will be prosecuted." In "Heaven Is a Busy Place" (252) his playful irreverence is never offensive; indeed after the initial shock of "Those in a state of grace / Continually twanging the harp" we see a simple piety emerging: "Sparrows to be watched as they fall, / Elephants, ants and all. . . ."

Stewart is the most spontaneous of poets: he rejoices in contemplating the simplest object of his poetry as much as the most complicated. Good moments occur frequently when one of his poems converts a nearly sentimental theme into something better, with a sharp, enlivening idea. He is never happier than when he is inside life, accepting rather than questioning all its values. Always in his poetry is humanity and a sensitive way with the details of day-to-day experience. Above all he has the ambition that his poetry should be enjoyed, and it is the ever-present spark of his humour that has, in fact, brought this to pass.

V *Love Poetry*

Stewart wrote once that the tolerance of maturity is not always to be preferred to the romantic ardor of youth.[31] It is a fact that almost all of his poetry that can be described as "love

poetry" is contained in the volumes of his verse published between 1936 and 1941. Stewart himself admits this.

... it's just natural when you're younger to be more passionate and
intense about everything, and it's the time when you go through your
love affairs and when you are first starting to battle with the world—
which is such an enormous fight when you're young. Then afterwards you come to terms with things and I think if you're going to
continue writing at all you've got to become more tolerant and
philosophical.[32]

Certainly there is passion and intensity strikingly apparent in
his earliest love poems. His imagery is often bizarre, wild, and
striking: "Harsh black mockery," "my mind's dark ocean,"
"chill vegetable lips," "in your flesh your tiger passions sleep."
Admittedly there is conventional early writing: "And so upon
your warm white breast I lie / In utter peace, in rich abandonment"—but there is also the moving simplicity of genuine
emotion:

> To you who have the calm of grass and earth
> But all the sea's blue fury in your eyes,
> To you upon whose flesh of creamy moonlight
> Pale-gold a memory of sunlight lies,
>
> I send this sheaf of roses and these colours,
> That when the cream rose dies, the blue fire dims,
> Remembering me, your cool soul may grow warm
> As sunlight warms the moonlight of your limbs.
> ("With a Sheaf of Cream Roses," 302)

One notes in these early poems a preoccupation, probably
influenced both by the symbolists and by Roy Campbell, with
color: "rosy languor," "dark silver as she floats," "honey-golden
throat," "pale-green star of woman," "creamy moonrose of
your limbs."
There is a haunting metaphysical quality in "The Mirror"
(271):

> The sharp clock speaking,
> Piercing, breaking

> The dark of dew and branches there:
> A woman in the mirror shaking
> Her starling-flying hair.

And yet in "A Summer Dusk" (283) there is an individual quality that could be ascribed to no influence other than the remarkable apprehension of a young poet rapidly developing his range of emotional, imaginative, even mystical experience:

> Come close, beloved, for the black wind swirls,
> The fire burns low, as quick as candles melt,
> And lonely in the shadows is your flute.
>
> You have yourself alone to light your route,
> Pale lilied flame, white wavering flute of light,
> And in dark woods a dark wind wails and whirls
>
> And I have seen the bodies of young girls
> As smooth as candles, as slender and as white,
> Go shrivelling into age as candles melt,
>
> And their gold faces gutter and go out,
> And their gold faces gutter and go out.
>
> (284)

Stewart's output of love poetry is chiefly contained (if we do not take the verse play *The Golden Lover* into account) in less than twenty poems from his earliest collections; none of them could be rated among his best work. Yet they remain as important proof that the poet's training period had included almost every facet of poetic experience, including the normal impulses of the young poet to sing of the mysteries and delights of love.

VI *Poems Descriptive of Australia*

Finally there remains a small but most important body of poetry wherein Stewart sets out to explore his adopted country. "Explore" is the operative word; it is not poetry written out of duty or obligation or gratitude but because as Stewart has said himself, "I have always had a curiosity about Australia."

There are odd poems where Stewart takes people and places commemorated in the average Australian's vision of her great outback—such as "The Man from Adaminaby" (69), "Mahony's Mountain" (168), "Murrumbidgee" (118), and his fantasy "The Bunyip" (226) (a mythical Australian creature, seallike in appearance, allegedly haunting swamps and streams) wherein Stewart indulges the riot of his imagination, perhaps with underlying meaning:

The kookaburra drank, he says, then shrieked at me with laughter,
I dragged him down in a hairy hand and ate his thighbones after;
My head is bruised with the falling foam, the water blinds my eye
Yet I will climb that waterfall and walk upon the sky.

(226)

But incomparably the best of his poetry about Australia rests in the sequence of twenty-seven poems entitled "The Birdsville Track." Its genesis is unusual. The Birdsville Track is a route stretching across the so-called "Dead Centre" of the great Australian continent, along the fringes of its great deserts. Stewart had always had a hankering to travel through the "Centre" and accepted an invitation from an Australian film-maker to write the script for a documentary film that the latter was making about this vast area. Stewart went on location and conceived the idea of the commentary as a series of poems— "a kind of incidental music with the desert scenery going on," as he described it. "When I saw the desert," he recalls, "it hit me like a thunderclap and I wrote these poems, most of them in the first draft and sometimes even completed, bouncing along in the mailman's truck over the desert in a temperature of over a hundred—I was just on fire with it. . . ."[33]

Of course his idea was in vain as far as the film was concerned—the producer wanted a commentary fitting the image in detail, so Stewart kept his poems for separate publication.[34] This was singularly fortunate, for the series represents the height of Stewart's achievement as a descriptive nature and lyric poet in all his methods of versification. Much of Stewart's poetry, like that of the best Australian poets such as the late Kenneth Slessor, Judith Wright, A. D. Hope, FitzGerald, and others, is never recognizably Australian in setting or in sentiment.

Stewart (as he proves in this sequence of poems) is quite capable of discovering the Australian reality in his own way, in his own terms, and, as it turned out, in his own good time (in fact seventeen years after he had made his home in Australia).

Nothing has escaped Stewart's poetic observation of the great Australian "dead heart." Images of the intense heat, the "red land," and the "vast hot plain" abound through his poems; his main symbol is the "red stones" ("the red stones bake," "the red stones glare"), which occurs in no less than eight of these poems.

There is good reason why Stewart should have found it appropriate to convey by such a graphic image the impression of burning heat he had himself experienced in the Australian inland. One is reminded of the entry in the journal of one of Australia's early explorers, Captain Charles Sturt, who had, like Stewart, traversed this area. He described how, at 127° Fahrenheit, his thermometer shattered, and his matches burst into flame when they fell to the ground.

... the blasts of heat were so terrific, that I wondered the very grass did not take fire ... everything, both animate and inanimate, gave way before it: the horses stood with their backs to the wind, and their noses to the ground, without the muscular strength to raise their heads; the birds were mute, and the leaves of the trees, under which we were sitting, fell like a snow shower around us ...[35]

With the heat comes drought and death, the twin and inevitable hazards of the Australian outback:

> There was no water on that plain
> But fire in stone and air
> Licking the cattle bones again
> That dingoes had picked bare.
> ("Blazes Well," 133)

> Where red stones burn and white stones flash
> Dead bullocks lie like living flesh;
> The dingo tunnels below the hide,
> Crow and eaglehawk work inside;

> Cleaned by the wind, by hot sun dried,
> With folded legs and heads turned back
> Just as they lived, just as they died,
> Hollow and gaunt and bony-eyed
> They stare along the Birdsville Track.
>   ("The Track Begins," 127)

Yet, the poet's eye sees and records the occasional flashes of more brilliant color among the drabs, duns, and dull reds of the desert country: "The cassia drinks the sky in its gold cup," "... the dwarf wild-hops lift up / Their tufts of crimson flame" (123), "the silver saltbush bubble." And here where "the world ends in a shield of purple stone" (123), Stewart writes too of the denizens of the center—the old camel driver, "the giant Afghan / Who steered his life by compass and by Koran" (126); the lonely Lutheran missionary, old Father Vogelsang, whose "sword flashed / In the sun as he dashed / Through the quarreling tribes" (137), and the aboriginals—the native tribes of Australia—whom Stewart has seen with compassion as well as with indignation:

> The blackfellow's squalid shanty
> Of rags and bags and tins,
> The bright-red dresses of the gins
> Flowering in that hot country
> Like lilies in the dust's soft pond.
>   ("Marree," 123)

Just as appealing to Stewart was the dour courage of the bush folk who, faced by heat, drought, and dust, have survived to eke out a sort of marginal existence. Their sardonic and fatalistic attitude to living and dying found a chord in the gentler irony with which Stewart himself surveys the world, and led him in this Birdsville sequence to commemorate the hardy philosophy of the men of the outback in a number of these poems, notably in "The Humorists" (which I have already quoted in Chapter 1).

Most of these poems have called on Stewart's lyrical and narrative skill; but it was impossble for him in his wanderings through this lonely land not to have found scope for his medi-

tative bent, as he has done in one of the finest poems of the
sequence, "Night Camp" (135). The form and rhythm he em-
ploys, the recondite (for the desert) imagery of surf and foam,
the tranquillity and peace conjured up in the last four lines
mark the heights of his poetic ability:

> Sleep, traveller, under the thorn on the stones.
> Somewhere on earth a man must lie down in trust
> And though behind you, cold as it breathes on your hand,
> Thudding like surf through the desert, foaming with dust,
> Rushes the wind that moves the hills of sand,
> What need of more than a bush to turn the gale?
> Sleep, all's well.
>
> Look where the dusty blossoms shake on the thorn
> Over your head, like motes in a shaft of the moon
> Climbing and falling, fluttering their wings now come
> Tiny white moths that call this desert home.

The coming of age of poetry in Australia in Stewart's generation has shown itself in the fact that its poets have ceased to be
self-consciously Australian. "Australianness," once a dominant
literary issue, is now no longer so. The Australian literary historian Cecil Hadgraft has written that poets in Australia may be
divided chronologically into English poets, Australian poets,
and poets.[36] The derivative mode was to be expected in the beginning; then, unexpectedly, the literary English manner of
describing Australia gave way to a more natural Australian manner. But now we have poets. There has been a spiritual development—a growing consciousness of an imaginative world, an
extension of the dimensions of experience. Australian poets,
especially those who are Stewart's contemporaries, have come
to understand more feelingly the problems of a transplanted culture; their poetry has become less "Australian" by being better
written. Stewart, like Judith Wright, A. D. Hope, and others,
has written much poetry which from its vocabulary, idiom,
and imagery could not be categorized as having been written
in any particular country. When occasionally these poets *have*
turned to some vividly imaginative experience of an Australian
background or scene it has been to demonstrate some universal

poetic truth. In the case of "The Birdsville Track," Stewart as part of *his* particular contribution to the rediscovery and reassessment of the whole Australian environment, has seized on the courage of the dwellers of the vast inland desert country in battling adversity and a perpetually hostile terrain, and he has made this the recurring theme of the sequence. If these people have not triumphed, he seems to be saying, at least they have survived by will and endurance; as he writes in "The Branding Fire" (139):

> Like smouldering coals I hear their laughter;
> Like man's own will I see that fire,
> Who stamps the stones with his desire,
> Who herds his beasts and burns his brand
> Like red-hot iron on this red land.

CHAPTER 3

Douglas Stewart as Verse Playwright

DOUGLAS Stewart is best known to his fellow Australians as a verse playwright, in particular as a radio dramatist. Whether his finest work as an Australian writer is as a verse playwright is for posterity to judge: I personally have no doubt that it is. Even Australia's most distinguished literary historian, H. M. Green, was prepared to state that Stewart's plays were "as good an illustration as his poems" of his varied talent.[1] But Stewart himself has underlined his popular success as a playwright with an amusing anecdote.[2] His first radio play, *The Fire on the Snow* (about Scott's ill-fated expedition to the South Pole in 1912), has been set as a text for English literature studies in secondary schools throughout Australia for many years now, and thus has been read and heard by hundreds of thousands of school children. Stewart was told that when young lifesavers in one of the many surf-clubs on Sydney beaches dive out of their boats into the deep ocean, it is customary for them to say "I am just going outside... I may be some time." These are the words of Captain Oates in the play. Stewart finds it a "curious and unnerving thought" that some of the words of his plays should have passed into the conversation of young Australians.

Altogether Stewart has written six verse plays. *The Fire on the Snow* was first performed by the Australian Broadcasting Commission (ABC) in 1941. It was written as a radio play, as was *The Golden Lover* (1943)—a play on the theme of Maori life and legend. *Ned Kelly* was intended as a stage play but had its first performance in an abbreviated text as a radio play in 1942. Its subject is the notorious Australian outlaw ("bushranger") who terrorized the districts of Southeastern Australia before he was captured and hanged in Melbourne in 1880. *The*

59

Earthquake Shakes the Land (about the Maori wars) was written as a radio play and first performed by the Australian Broadcasting Commission in 1944. *Shipwreck* (1947), which centers
about incidents during the period when the Dutch explorer
Francis Pelsart's ship *Batavia* was wrecked in 1629 on one of
the islands off the West Coast of Australia (now known as
Pelsart's Abroholos), was writtten as a stage play, as was *Fisher's Ghost* (1960), described as an "Historical Comedy." All
the plays, with the exception of *The Earthquake Shakes the
Land,* have been published in book form.

I   Origins of the Radio Verse Play

While it is not my concern to delve too deeply into the history
of the verse play as such in English literature, it is safe to say
that after the decline of the Elizabethan-Jacobean drama this
genre had little conspicuous success up to the turn of the present
century. Dull curiosities like Addison's *Cato* and Johnson's
Irene in the eighteenth century were succeeded in the nine-
teenth century by scarcely more inspiring efforts from Byron,
Coleridge, Tennyson, and Browning. There was dramatic fire
in Shelley's *Cenci*, admittedly, but it was the twentieth century
which saw more horsepower injected into the genre with the
experiments of W. B. Yeats; the notable success of Flecker's
Hassan (1922), hailed by some as the most arresting verse drama
since John Webster wrote; the writings of John Masefield in
this form; and the ground which Sean O'Casey broke with
The Silver Tassie (1929) and *Within the Gates* (1933) in his
efforts to turn the sods for new ways in drama.

These latter experiments are not without significance in the
birth of radio verse drama as a popular and influential literary
form. The British Broadcasting Corporation (BBC), set up in
1922, was by the early 1930's a significant enough annex of
England's cultural establishment to house many brilliant young
writers. They were to sow the seeds from which the many
glorious harvests of the Third Programme would be reaped in
the next and subsequent decades. Foremost among these was a
Lancashireman, D. G. Bridson, who had begun writing for the
BBC in 1933, joined its staff two years later, and being himself

a keen student of such contemporary verse drama as was being written, saw clearly the potential of radio for popular verse drama. Bridson not only understood that programs assimiliated through the ear could command a high degree of educated appreciation among responsible minorities—he took this for granted. He realized further that the wildfire spread of radio in a country of high-density population revealed a vast, receptive audience which would enable him, as he has put it, "to do for radio something comparable in its way to what had been done for the cinema by D. W. Griffith or Cecil B. De Mille."[3] He saw the challenge of telling dramatic stories, panoramic in scope; to make them more immediately exciting than anything that had been heard before; in so doing, to involve his listeners emotionally; to make them grip their chairs, as it were, and get caught in the action. And for this purpose he was convinced that verse could be made exciting, could bring about a more intense feeling of personal involvement, than prose. The result was his moving and inspired story of the Jacobite rebellion, *The March of the '45*, still the greatest radio verse play in our literature.

From it ultimately stemmed the many fine works that followed in this genre all over the world. Two of the most famous of these were *The Fall of the City* and *Christopher Columbus;* in the preface to the former, its author, the American Archibald MacLeish, hailed Bridson's play as its prototype; the poet Louis MacNeice, author of the latter, paid a similar handsome tribute. Bridson followed his original source with a string of brilliant radio verse dramas on the BBC, perhaps the two most outstanding of which were *Aaron's Field* and *The Quest of Gilgamesh*. Literature was enriched with many others of the type that followed in these golden years of radio. I need only mention Maxwell Anderson's *Winterset*, Eric Linklater's *Socrates Asks Why*, Louis MacNeice's *The Dark Tower*, Laurie Lee's *Voyage of Magellan*, Henry Reed's *Streets of Pompeii*, David Jones's *In Parenthesis* and of course Dylan Thomas's *Under Milk Wood*, perhaps the one play which merits comparison with Bridson's *The March of '45*. In Canada, CBC radio also experimented successfully with verse drama. Early productions in this genre by Lister Sinclair led to further writing by poets such as Phyllis Gotlieb, Gwendolyn MacEwen, and Margaret Atwood. In recent years John Reeves, a CBC drama producer, has had notable successes with his verse plays and in 1959 won the Prix Italia with his production of his own play "The Last Summer of Childhood."

It is relevant too, I think, to this great achievement of Bridson, that since his play had been first performed in 1933, was repeated several times within the next year or two, and evoked unanimous praise in literary circles of the day, its influence was directly or indirectly to be seen in the renascence of the verse play proper in the pre–World War II years. T. E. Eliot wrote *Murder in the Cathedral* in 1935, and Auden and Isherwood *The Ascent of F6* in 1936. The later Eliot verse plays and Christopher Fry's *The Lady's Not for Burning* and *A Phoenix Too Frequent* continued these remarkable attempts (even if concentrated over a relatively short period of literary history) to reconcile poetry with the practical demands of the theater. And so it followed that once this aim was accomplished, audiences as well as readers were the richer in their theatrical and emotional experiences.

In the case of the radio plays I have mentioned, many of them were published in book form, and many were also heard all over the English-speaking world through the BBC Transcription Service or performed by local radio players from the original scripts. And in Australia a young poet pricked up his ears and listened.

II *Influences on Douglas Stewart as Radio Verse Dramatist*

Stewart frankly admits[4] that though he had heard of Bridson he had not listened to any of his plays before he came to write *The Fire on the Snow* for its first performance in 1941. This is not surprising since radio listening in Australia in the Depression years was not a general experience, and Stewart himself did not listen much to radio at the time and, if anything, rather despised it as a medium.[5] He had, however, read *The Ascent of F6*, which he did not like, and *Murder in the Cathedral*, which he greatly admired. "From it arose the whole modern movement in verse drama," he wrote subsequently,[6] and he offered the further observation after reading *The Cocktail Party* that "it is possible that the simple device where the poetry lies not in the words but in the rhythm, may be Eliot's most important contribution to the renascence of the poetic drama."[7] But it was not contemporary verse drama that sparked off his first achievement. After all, he had read Shakespeare enthusiastically in his student days, as well as the plays of other Elizabethan and later dramatists. *The Duchess of Malfi* was one of his especial favorites (a point which I find of incidental interest since the lines about Oates, perished in the snow, "That look in his eyes, fire ice jewels," have a striking parallel with "Cover her face, mine eyes dazzle, she died young").

The fact was that Stewart carried the idea of *The Fire on the Snow* around for six or seven years, trying to write it as a narrative poem "and not being able to find a key to get the thing going."[8] He was aware implicity of all the difficulties that faced him if he essayed the verse drama form. Just to write excellent poetry was not enough. As Shelley had found with *The Cenci* it had to be different verse. As verse it had to be subordinated to the dramatic form; spoken and listened to for long periods its rhythms as well as its meaning had to be clear. Ordinary human speech had to come through in simple, everyday terms and yet there had to be opportunities for the most noble flights of imagination and the expression of intense emotions. Character in action must emerge, a most difficult undertaking in the verse form, and above all the happenings of an event in 1912 had to be given appropriate relevance to contemporary moods, to attitudes of Australians thirty years later. But when Stewart first heard *The Fall of the City,* he found the key—the "great discovery,"[9] as he calls it—the Announcer, and that all could be linked together by the Announcer.

But there still remained the problem of the verse form and here Stewart had done his homework, as his fellow countrymen would say. He had always been a student of speech rhymes, and as well as his own experiments in metrical forms he had made a hobby of noting down any unusual aspects of the everyday talk of people he met and associated with. He once argued with his fellow poet Kenneth Slessor for the five hours of a motor car trip from Sydney to Canberra about the correct scansion of two lines of verse;[10] he had a theory too that most people, when their emotions were aroused, talked poetry without knowing it. He illustrated this once in the course of a lively essay entitled "Tricks of the Trade."[11]

I once heard a man speaking of his home in the country: "The air's so clear—ten miles away at night you can hear the whistle and the train coming into the station. You can hear it going away to Brisbane in the night, and that's ten miles away." Then he went on to rage against the city: "You can feel the air all thick with the people tramping the bitumen up off the roads."

He was speaking with emotion; and, in a line of five stresses, he was talking a quite tolerable poetry:

> The *air's* so *clear*—ten *miles* a*way* at *night*
> You can *hear* the *whis*tle, and the *train* coming *into* the *sta*tion.

> You can *hear* it *going* a*way* to *Bris*bane in the *night*,
> And *that's* ten *miles* a*way*.

> You can *feel* the *air* all *thick* with the *peo*ple *tramp*ing
> The *bit*umen *up* off the *roads*.

That is the natural speech rhythm on which all the academic measures of poetry are based. It is the rhythm of the awakened emotions, like the beat of the heart. If you listen for it carefully you will hear it nearly always when people are recalling the cherished scenes of childhood; and it lends a pleasing dignity to household quarrels to know that they are usually conducted in a blank verse of five stresses per line.

Stewart thus found the ideal medium which would enable him to widen the horizons of acceptance of poetic form among people who would not normally wish to be exposed to it; who indeed would be embarrassed to do so. (The Australian radio audience of the early 1940's was far less culturally sophisticated than the British audience of even a decade previously.) He preferred, as part of his approach, to regard his five-stress line as an iambic pentameter modified by natural rhythm, or a line of natural rhythm modified by the iambic pentameter.

Once he had written *The Fire on the Snow* Stewart became passionately interested in the verse play. The Australian Broadcasting Commission employed him to adapt plays by Shakespeare,

Marlowe, Webster—even Shelley's *The Cenci* and Browning's *The Ring and the Book*—for radio. He found this a splendid discipline—it also did wonders for his verse technique. As he recalls, "I found it invaluable in learning the principles on which a play, or any genuine work of creative literature, is constructed. It has, strange to say, a beginning, a middle and an end; and when you are cutting a three hour stage play down to an hour for radio, you must cut to that line."[12]

He turned to the Greek dramatists, like Euripides, and read them voraciously, even, as he recollects, in bed in the small hours of the night.[13] He turned again to the poets who used blank verse individually and characteristically: Whitman with his alleged "free verse" poured out in lines of seven stresses; Hopkins with his notions of "hangers" and "outriders" as devices to disregard unstressed syllables; Bridges with his use of the same principle under the name of "sprung rhythms."

Thus he was able to vary his stance, as it were. In *Ned Kelly* he interspersed his blank verse with the ordinary prose speech of his characters when emotion or action or, indeed, poetry, demanded it. In *Fisher's Ghost* he used a lighter verse, with a sprinkling of Australian ballad style as befitted a merry romp about a fairly affable ghost. In his Maori plays he achieved astonishing flexibility in embodying the parry and thrust of the speech patterns of his characters. But above all, Stewart appreciated from the beginning that if a verse play was to be written in Australia which could be comparable with *The Fall of the City* or even *Murder in the Cathedral*, it had to be good verse and a good play, the two things judged separately and judged together.

In all this Stewart succeeded beyond his expectations. And before I turn to an analysis of his plays individually, it is necessary to say that he inspired a whole movement of radio verse playwriting among his contemporaries, even though most of them fell short of their exemplar. But some deserve mention. Inspired by the success of *The Fire on the Snow* the Australian Broadcasting Commission conducted a verse play competition which produced two notable successes: *We're Going Through* by T. Inglis Moore (the theme was the heroic deeds of Australians during the fighting against the Japanese, vigorously

and challengingly presented) and *The Path of the Eagle,* a
psychological drama by Catherine Duncan. Later the now-
famous Australian novelist Morris West wrote *The Illusionists,*
on the theme of the dilemma of an artist hesitating between
commercial and artistic success. Kenneth Mackenzie's emotional
Young Shakespeare and Shan Benson's *Voyage on a Dinner
Table,* a radio portrait of Captain Cook, also made a sharp
impact at the time. Even though, as in England, the tide of
this particular type of creative activity ebbed within a decade
or so (radio plays are invariably in prose nowadays), it is
Douglas Stewart's achievement that singlehandedly he pioneered
one of the most memorable bursts of creative activity in Australian literary history.

III   *The Verse Dramas*

A   *The Fire on the Snow*

Australia has but two hundred years of history to fall back
on and some of its early bloodstained episodes of convict settlement and aboriginal genocide are best forgotten. Consequently
the average Australian surveying his country's achievements
takes the more conscious pride in the deeds of the great explorers like Burke and Wills, Leichhardt, Captain Sturt, and others
who in the burning deserts and inhospitable bush land of
Australia's vast interior, made their heroic and, in some cases,
tragic journeys. In this century Australia had a stake too in the
exploration of one of the last challenges to man in the Southern
Hemisphere—the Antarctic and the South Pole.

Antarctica's geographical proximity to Australia, which inevitably served as a jumping-off point even for expeditions
arriving from overseas, has added to a sense of national involvement. And when Douglas Stewart's radio play *The Fire on
the Snow* was first performed in 1941, its audience would have
included many Australians who had personal memories of some
of the most dramatic of these Antarctic explorations. Two distinguished Australians, Professor (later Sir) Edgeworth David
and Dr. (later Sir) Douglas Mawson played a leading part in
Sir Ernest Shackleton's desperate but unsuccessful bid to reach
the South Pole in 1908. Mawson later became the first Aus-

tralian to lead an Antarctic expedition when in 1912 he carried out an exciting and adventurous exploration. His book *The Home of the Blizzard*, telling of his exploits, became an Australian classic and earned for Mawson the admiration and indeed reverence of his fellow countrymen during his lifetime. He was still alive (he died in 1958) when Stewart's play was first performed. Captain Robert Scott's 1911 expedition included three Australians in one of the scientific parties attached to the main group, and when Sir Ernest Shackleton led another expedition to the Antarctic in 1914, again three Australians were included, among them the famous war photographer J. F. Hurley, whose photographs of this expedition are still preserved on exhibition in Australian galleries.

Undoubtedly then Douglas Stewart had a theme ready-made for success. The tragic heroism of Captain Scott had, in any case, touched the emotions of Australians just as much as of his English countrymen. Scott with four companions had made a desperate dash by sledge for the South Pole in November 1911. They were delayed by bad weather, and when they reached the Pole after appalling privations they found they had been beaten there by the Norwegian explorer Amundsen only a few days before. Shatteringly disappointed and desperately weary they set back on the return journey, slowed down by sickness, insufficiency of food, and continued severe weather. Petty Officer Edgar Evans died under the strain. Four weeks later Captain L. E. G. Oates, who was too ill to travel further, walked out into a blizzard hoping by his sacrifice to save his companions. But the weather closed in, and a few days later the party pitched its final camp. There are many Australians of adult age who know by heart Scott's last tragic entry in his diary, dated March 29, 1912.

Every day we have been ready to start for our depot 11 miles away but outside the door of the tent it remains a scene of whirling drift. . . . We shall stick it out to the end, but we are getting weaker of course, and the end cannot be far. It seems a pity but I do not think I can write any more. . . .

Eight months later a search party found Scott's tent with his body and those of his two remaining companions, E. A. Wilson

and Lieutenant H. R. Bowers; thirty pounds of valuable geo-
logical specimens that the party had hauled to the very last
(one of the sublimest actions of the whole journey); and
Scott's records and diaries which gave a full account of the
journey. These were later published as *Scott's Last Expedition*,
edited by Leonard Huxley, and along with Apsley Cherry-
Garrard's *The Worst Journey in the World* they were the basic
source materials used by Douglas Stewart to write his play.

Stewart succeeded brilliantly; *The Fire on the Snow*,* as
Leslie Rees, Australia's leading drama authority, has written, is

a classic of southern literature and will remain so ... a theme,
heroic endurance unto death; a form, the continually moving single
scene—that is, moving through time *and* space—indigenous to radio
and not suitable for stage; a command over verse varying from
colloquial exchanges between the five men on the ice to the narrator's finely sculptured comments, heavy with fate; and a gift for
conveying the most poignant human emotion.[14]

It has been broadcast many times by the Australian Broad-
casting Commission; it was the first Australian radio verse play
to be accepted and broadcast by the British Broadcasting
Corporation; it has also been broadcast in Canada, Japan, South
Africa, New Zealand, Norway and Denmark, and even in
Iceland.

When one considers that Stewart had not written a radio
play before, his skill in coping with its peculiarities is the more
remarkable. First of all, having seized on the idea of the Announcer, he unerringly thereby confirmed the "broadcast" character of the play. It was not enough to regard the Announcer
merely as a chorus "to break into the conversation, with a word
that tastes like snow..." or "to interrupt the contemplation,
of the familiar headlines of the day" (3). Rather Stewart used
the device actively, dynamically. The Narrator, for instance, sets
out the theme of the quest:

---

* For quotations that follow from this and other plays except *Fisher's
Ghost* and *The Earthquake Shakes the Land* (which was never pub-
lished), page references are given for *Four Plays*, by Douglas Stewart
(Sydney, 1958).

> But the reply comes: the world is spun
> Between two giant hands of ice.
> And on any peak of living won
> From hardest hours, the blizzard's hiss.
> And the reward set for the blindest faith
> In the fixed needle directing us
> Is to reach the Pole; and the Pole to death.
>
> (4)

In a context where like the Elizabethan drama there is no limitation on space, through which a single scene moves unfettered also by the limitation of time, Stewart uses the Announcer to describe the scenery and, when necessary, to carry the action along:

> . . . I see them hauling
> Grimly, not talking much, then making camp.
> Evans, the giant worker, has cut his hand
> But still attends to the sledges, pitches the tent,
> The strongest man of the party.
>
> (7–8)

If the Announcer is, sometimes prosaically, the bare commentator, this is richly redeemed when Stewart puts into his mouth words of purest poetry, as where musing on the delight of achievement, he continues:

> The delight is a moment's delight, it will die at the
>   moment of knowing
> That a man lies dead on the snow and another
>   man steps are slowing
> And the barren plain has no end and the iron
>   wind is blowing.
>
> (17)

Never at any time, however, does Stewart allow himself through this device to fall into the twin pits of flashback and reminiscence; furthermore, the verse of the Announcer's speech is invariably clean, sparse, and hard, thus giving an incisiveness to the story and serving also structurally to balance the play.

Secondly, in a radio play the characters must be made to

come to life in the imagination. There has been some criticism
of the play's weakness in establishing a "clear, distinct inter-
relation"[15] between the characters; this observation seems to
me, however, to lose sight of the radio producer's important
function to cast the play effectively with the necessary contrast
in, and individuality of, voicing. But in any case it is my view
that Stewart's script does *not* fail in this essential. Scott is the
heroic leader dauntlessly optimistic till the very end,

> (The will to triumph
> Brought us this dreadful journey, the will to live
> Must see us home again . . .).
>
> (13)

who, in his last words with Wilson, yields to none in his praise
of his men

> I have said so in my diary. It will be found
> And people will know some day that Bowers was a hero
> And Oates walked to death like a god and Evans was strong.
> They'll know too how much your friendship has meant.
>
> (28)

Wilson, the scientist and academic, who finds courage in his
own philosophy and learning, emerges no less clearly as an
individual:

> When a man is calmly dying, you do nothing
> But watch the tide go out, wait for the last
> Lap of the heart, ripple of light in the eyes,
> Then you go home.
>
> (16)

So it is too with the gallant Oates, the faithful and strong
seaman, Evans, the generous but impatient Bowers. It is a great
triumph for Stewart to have achieved this differentiation.

Above all there is the pure poetry of the play which, coming
via the microphone, enriches all those within the loudspeaker's
range with the intensity of the emotion it expresses, with its
precise conjunction of form and meaning—a poetry that yet is

made for speaking. Oates "walking on ice, walking in the whiter / Exaltation of death," or the Announcer's description of the all-pervading silence of the icy wastes which ". . . the natural growth of the hardy country / Rears like a winter tree among them, implacable," or the heartbreaking nostalgia of Scott's vision of his beloved London as he faces the eight hundred impossible miles back to base. . . .

> I like to think of the lights of Piccadilly
> And of how in the smoky Park among the oaks
> All London suddenly breaks on you like thunder.
>
> (12)

These are jewels of verse that glitter like the ice of the terrain with which the play is concerned.

There is indeed a simple poetic dignity in much of Scott's Diary which any writer would find it hard to improve upon. Yet as an illustration of Stewart's consummate craftsmanship and of the manner in which he has imaginatively but always with dignity and unerring good taste, embellished his sources in his creation of dialogue and his need to maintain motivation, action, and above all dramatic suspense, I offer this comparison of Scott's moving yet magnificent entry recording Oates's death, with the Stewart interpretation.

The original reads:

Should this be found I want these facts recorded. Oates' last thoughts were of his Mother, but immediately before he took pride in thinking that his regiment would be pleased with the bold way in which he met his death. We can testify to his bravery. He has borne intense suffering for weeks without complaint, and to the very last was able and willing to discuss outside subjects. He did not—would not— give up hope to the very end. He was a brave soul. This was the end. He slept through the night before last, hoping not to wake; but he woke in the morning—yesterday. It was blowing a blizzard. He said, "I am just going outside and may be some time." He went out into the blizzard and we have not seen him since.[16]

Stewart's interpretation is as follows:

Oates.   I had hoped not to wake this morning. It's cold.
A blizzard outside?

Scott.   A blizzard. We must march if we can.

Oates.   I'm glad there's a blizzard. The sunlight here's
too cruel,
Lighting the ice and everything looking naked.
When it's grey and snowy it makes me think of home,
I suppose because of December and the fires.
I see my mother quite clearly, lighting the sticks,
Stooping, as over the garden in the summer.
Colours and flowers and flames come out of her hands.
There were good days in the regiment, too, in winter.
Hard, brisk days and wine at night
And the horses steaming and bucking on frosty mornings
It's good to have lived.

Bowers.   Good to be living, too.
We'll make it yet.

Oates.   Living is over for me.

Wilson.   Wait till the doctor tells you, Soldier. Hardly
Thirty more miles and we'll be at One Ton Camp.
Cherry and the dogs'll be there and we'll haul you home
Like a prince, lying back on the sledge and watching the scenery.

Oates.   Don't. Don't, Wilson. You only make it
Harder, for me and for all of us. No more pretending.

Scott.   At lunch-time yesterday you thought you couldn't go on
Yet you managed to march, and the same can be done to-day.

Oates.   And to-morrow? And the day after that? No.
Not even to-day.

Bowers.   I'll help you along.

Oates.   Thank you. You're all very kind. Too kind
To a man who's been a burden these past three weeks.
Too kind, too kind.

Scott.   Soldier!
What are you doing? For Christ's sake, where are you
Going?

Wilson.   You mustn't! Bowers, hold him! Hold him.

Bowers. Soldier, you fool, it's blowing hell outside,
    A howling blizzard.

Oates.   Nobody move, don't move.
    I am just going outside. I may be some time.

                    The Announcer
    They let him go.
    In grief and shame
    They let him go
        Out to the flame
    Of wind and snow
    Where he burns for them.

                                        (21–22)

It is hardly necessary to reiterate the devices of poetry employed by Stewart in his elaboration of Scott's simple diary
entry: they are there for the reading; but most notable and
effective is Stewart's conversion of Oates's last words into two
short, powerful, and pregnant sentences.

So much for Stewart's mastery of the radio play at his first
attempt. But *The Fire on the Snow* is, more importantly, the
means whereby Stewart was able to begin to put into poetry
some of his attitudes to life: his observations of the preoccupations and aspirations of men. Certain of these themes, as we
shall see, run through a number of his plays. Neither in his
verse up to this time nor in that which has followed since he
ceased to write plays, could he be regarded as a symbolist. His
poems do not convey messages. But in his plays it is as if he
saw opportunity and perhaps even incentive to develop his
awareness of the forces that direct, even impel, men and women
to behave as they do.

Foremost in *The Fire on the Snow* is his consciousness of the
contrast between the dream and the reality. Indeed the essence
of this play, despite subsidiary themes which are developed,
is the shattering of a dream in the most tragic and pitiable of
circumstances. Scott first admits to his dream when in dis-
appointment but not in dejection he sees Amundsen's black
Norwegian flag planted at the Pole:

I've dreamed of this moment for many, many years
But the dream was different, no footsteps scarring the snow,
No mark of men.

(12)

Yet, he will not be robbed of his achievement; he is where he
planned to be. But it is when he speaks brave words to his
companions against the "dreadful journey" which faces them,
that the cold, detached voice of the Announcer breaks in,

They turn their backs on the Pole
They turn their backs on a dream
(13)

and the truth—the knowledge that it was, after all, a dream,
one man's dream—is upon us. And when Evans freezes to a
terrible death, it is the Announcer again who voices this truth:

This journey is one man's dream
As it is one man's burden
And the man is Scott, the leader.
The others do what they're bidden,
Bearing their share of the load,
But cannot tell what it means.
Evans, who understood least,
Was the first to die, a man
Lost in a nightmare, lost
In the fog of another man's dream.
(16)

Then, when Oates too is dead, again Stewart turns to the
Announcer in poetry where repetition tolls like a knell to voice
the reality:

Sick with the sight of death and numb with the knowledge
Of almost certain death in the blizzard ahead
They have been out on the ice more than a hundred days
They have marched on the ice for over a thousand miles.
They saw their dream topple and crash like a wave
And waste itself on the bitter shore of the Pole.
(23)

At the moment of death it is left to the scholar and philosopher Wilson, alone of all the characters to restate the dream, its shattering and yet what may be pieced together from the fragments:

> We dreamed, we so nearly triumphed, we were defeated
> As every man in some great or humble way
> Dreams, and nearly triumphs, and is always defeated,
> And then, as we did, triumphs again in endurance.
>
> (30)

The Australian poet and scholar James McAuley has noted[17] another aspect of the play's theme—the question of leadership. Scott, as the Announcer has said, is the leader, "The others do what they're bidden"; he is the master.

> As every dreamer has been
> Who ruled men's minds or bodies
> Who had no will of their own.
>
> (17)

But McAuley makes the interesting observation that at the end of the play "Wilson in a passage which also carries authority, asserts a view which seems incompatible with this: instead of the image of the leader animating the inert, we are given the image of a community of men, each finding his own personal meaning and motive and making his choice:

> All of us chose to do it,
> Our own will brought us, our death on the ice
> was foreseen by each of us: accepted.
>
> (29)

But there is no sign that this clash of interpretations is fully meant, or worked out dramatically. That is to say, the Scott-Announcer view is not tested *against* the Wilson view or reconciled with it."

It seems to me, however, that the most magnificently sustained symbolism in the play is that conveyed in the title itself. The fire on the snow is the courage and endurance of Scott and his

men, the saga of personal heroism that will remain in human
memory for as long as the records are kept. Fire as the symbol
of fortitude is maintained consistently yet with poetic unob-
trusiveness throughout the play. Stewart thereby creates a sort
of magic—we accept the proposition without question and as
suffering and death occur (something which would be almost
pointless in any other context—as pointless indeed as the use
of violence as a theme in a 1974 movie film) our emotions are
kept in a constant state of exhilaration. We are made aware
toward the end of the play that the capacity of man to endure
beyond the sticking-place, as it were, is to Scott almost the
Holy Grail, yet there is no hint of masochism in this:

> a man must learn
> To endure agony, to endure and endure again
> Until agony itself is beaten out into joy.
>
> (28)

Wilson, the nearest to poet in the party, is Stewart's chosen
instrument to give imaginative assent to Scott's credo in terms
of the title's symbolism; Stewart has Wilson continually seeming
to be casting around for the philosopher's stone of poetry to
transmute Scott's prosaic, soldierly concept of the ultimate in
man's behavior into the fiery gold of the deathless human spirit.
Thus, after the death of Evans, Wilson gropes for the metaphor
when he says:

> Endurance may have a meaning
> For men in the snow as for saints and martyrs in flames.
>
> (20)

But then he gets nearer the poetic mark when he talks of the
"bitter process / That refines the soul in labour and flame."
Finally, with his dying words, he is able triumphantly to
crystallize the thought in what are some of Stewart's finest lines:

> And whenever death is
> The endurance remains like fire, a sculpture, a mountain
> To hearten our children. I tell you

> Such a struggle as ours is living; it lives after death
> Purely, like flame, a thing burning and perfect.
>
> (30)

But Stewart is not content to pursue his symbol only in these terms. What he does in addition is little short of poetic genius: he practices a fascinating counterpoint throughout the play, imperceptibly, indeed subliminally, injecting into his listeners' and readers' minds the antithetical symbolism of ice and flame. As Leslie Rees has observed, we have continually contrasted "the frozen rigour of the task and the fire of men's hardihood so that the text leaps and flashes with colour and sense-feeling, freezing and blazing."[18] To make the point arithmetically, Stewart in the space of an hour's text uses words or phrases denoting flame and fire twenty-two times. The first reference is simple (and subtle) enough—"the aurora leaps and towers / Colouring the Antarctic sky with terror." But gradually the antithesis becomes part of the warp and weft of the play. The men are "like dark tough flames on the snow." Scott sees "the moon come up from the shoulder of Erebus / and set the snow on fire." Oates, in the words of the Announcer already quoted, goes

> Out to the flame
> Of wind and snow
> Where he burns for them.
>
> (22)

Scott, with a burst of poetic expression that is the most telling (and beautiful) Stewart allows him, tells of a unique experience:

> One night I walked to the cliffs alone, and the moon
> Was pure and burning on those frozen spires and crags,
> So that they leapt like flames. The ice was blazing,
> And the hut, when I came back, was a red island,
> A ship at sea, a fire of human beings,
> Warm and secure.
>
> (29)

And at the end Scott's last words, the last words of the play, confirm the fusion of the impossible—fire and ice:

                            a dying man remembering
            The burning snow, the crags towering like flame.
                                                (30)

B. *Ned Kelly*

A "bushranger" is the Australian equivalent of an "outlaw"
or "highwayman." Since Australia began as a convict colony
it is not surprising that it has a quite imposing list of lawless
celebrities who can be compared with the Jesse Jameses and
Dick Turpins of other countries. And no less in Australia, some
of these bushrangers have achieved the status of folk heroes.

In its first forty or fifty years of settlement, escaped convicts
preyed on early colonists and settlers; this was especially the
case in the early 1800s. But the main phase of this type of
lawlessness began in the 1850s after the discovery of gold in
Australia—and the names of bushrangers operating in Eastern
parts of Australia in these years are now legendary: Ben Hall,
Frank Gardiner, Daniel Morgan, "Captain Thunderbolt" (Fred-
erick Ward), and one or two others. There followed a period
of relative quiet until the mid-1870s, when the exploits of
Ned Kelly and his gang, along the border country between
Victoria and New South Wales, captured the nation's attention.

Ned Kelly was the son of an Irish convict, transported to
Tasmania for attempts to shoot his landlord. In 1871, at the age
of seventeen, he was imprisoned for horse-stealing; his two
brothers, Jim and Dan, also served sentences of various terms.
Eventually in 1878 Ned formed the "Kelly Gang"—his accomplices were his brother Dan, Steve Hart, and Joe Byrne. After
several raids on homesteads and townships, the gang ambushed
and shot dead three policemen. Rewards "alive or dead" were
set on the men, and thus outlawed, they began a career even
more notorious.

Douglas Stewart's play is concerned with the gang from
the time of its most remarkable exploit—the "holding up" of
the bank at a small New South Wales town called Jerilderie in
February 1879 (where they held the population captive for
three days), and from which point the rewards on their heads
totalled £8,000 (about $100,000 in our terms). The gang then
laid low for several months, during which time they killed an

accomplice named Aaron Sherritt, turned police informer. Eventually they made their last stand in a town called Glenrowan, where they "interned" the entire male population in the local hotel and tore up the railway lines in a bid to wreck a police train which they knew was on its way to capture them. The local schoolmaster escaped from the hotel and stopped the train in time. A fullscale attack was made on the hotel. Kelly, clad in homemade armor (fashioned from parts of a stolen plow) allowed his captives to leave the hotel, and recklessly tried to shoot it out with the police in the open. He was wounded in the legs and captured; the hotel was set on fire and the bodies of his three accomplices (who had probably committed suicide) incinerated therein. Kelly was taken to Melbourne, tried, convicted of murder, and hanged on November 11, 1880.

The memory of his brutal deeds has long since faded: he has become perhaps the leading figure in Australian folklore; around his name ballads and melodramas have been composed and written. He has become the archetype for the Australian concept of daring and reckless bravery: "as game as Ned Kelly" is part of the language. Kelly's famous (but probably apocryphal) last words before he was hanged, "Such is life!" have also added to the legend, investing him with some added quality of saintliness.

Stewart's play, beginning as I have said with the Jerilderie bank robbery, ends with his capture at Glenrowan. It is made up of four acts. The first is taken up with the robbery of the bank at Jerilderie and the action, in two scenes, is spread over the three days' "siege" of the town, where, in their contact with various citizens such as Tarleton the bank manager, Gribble the clergyman, Cox the hotel keeper, Elliott the schoolteacher, we see the characters of the various members of the gang taking shape. The second act is set in the mountain ranges where the bushrangers have their fastness. It comprises one scene only; we see tensions developing among the men, and they are visited by The Kangaroo or the 'Roo, Ned Kelly's mistress. She tells them that Aaron Sherritt has informed on them, and is leading the police ("the traps") toward their hiding place. The third act has its first scene set in Sherritt's home; there is almost unbearable suspense as he talks with his wife and mother-in-law and the sergeant of police placed there to guard him. Sherritt, at the end of the scene, is lured out by the Kellys and shot. The short second scene transfers the action to Glenrowan, where the bushrangers destroy the railway line. The three scenes of the final act play out the end of the drama at the hotel where the bushrangers meet their death.

Depending on his interpretation of the Kellys' story—whether the emphasis should be upon the psychological factors of poverty and police oppression in turning Kelly and his brothers to crime; whether more attention should have been paid to the influences of his mother and sister, whom Stewart does not even introduce into the play; whether the play could have begun more effectively than with the Jerilderie episode; and so on— each reader could probably put his finger on some apparent structural weakness in the play. For my part, I find the first two scenes too long and wordy—they occupy over a third of the total length of the play—so that balance seems never to be quite restored. But I believe this and any other criticism is carping when the sweep and detail of the Kelly story is considered. Stewart's problem is not only in presenting a total effect of unity, but also in selecting those aspects of the story which would give free reign to his poetic urgings. This is Stewart's triumph, that *Ned Kelly* emerges as a sustained piece of poetic writing of the highest order. Furthermore, as his fellow poet and critic Nancy Keesing has said, "Its interpretation of Australian landscape was the most exhilarating and illuminating of any in our poetry until its time."[19]

Especially in the first act Stewart mixes ordinary prose with verse in the dialogue of his characters. He explains this by a definition he made for himself: "poetry is the natural speech of the aroused emotions";[20] hence he has his *dramatis personae* speak in verse when their emotions are stirred up, and then drop back to prose. He points out that people do this in life— "You can listen and hear them speaking poetry for quite a long time when they're aroused."[21] He has frequently developed this point. Some years after he had written his early verse plays he wrote of Shakespeare's use of language: "It is when his characters are most themselves, when they speak most forcibly in character, that their words are set out in prose. But when characters are most themselves, and are speaking with passion, that is the very time when they are likely to talk poetry."[22] As for the verse itself, it can easily be seen how Stewart has benefited from his experience in writing *The Fire on the Snow*. Take this passage from Act II, where Kelly emphasizes to his mates the loyalty of the bush people around them and the common hatred of "the traps":

> There's more than the Kellys
> Round Greta and Beechworth who don't want the snooping traps
> Poking their noses in; not just the duffers,
> There's plenty who're on the square but still remember
> It was traps who sent their fathers out to Australia
> For poaching a rabbit, stealing a loaf of bread—
> They're all for us: and there's others who never learned
> The limp of the lag, who'd like to see Australia
> A man's country, where the bush is left to itself
> And a colt that cuts up rough is liked for its spirit.

(169)

Stewart has developed, because he is dealing not with educated Englishmen but scarcely literate bushmen, a flexible, rolling line, loosely constructed (as can be seen by the second line in the quotation), which absorbs slang and imagery alike, keeping fundamentally to the five stresses even though it is difficult to scan as obviously pentametric. It is his version of the "poetry that people speak," a rhythmic speech completely acceptable to actors and hearers alike, hearers who, as Stewart has put it, would run a mile rather than listen to poetry.[23] The advance he has made in his craft is clearly discernible; the flexibility he accomplishes within his metrical discipline is at times breathtakingly effective as we can see in a passage where the anguished Byrne boggles at the prospect of killing the blacktrackers on their trail:

Byrne. . . .
     You want it again, murder piled on murder.
     How many? ——

Hart.   But listen, Joe ——

Dan.   He's crazy.

Ned.   Joe ⸺

Byrne (rushing from the room). I won't do it. Why did I ever do it?
         O God, what a life to live!
         (he goes.)

Dan (calling after him).   You'll be back.

Hart. With the traps and Aaron Sherritt.

Ned (heavily).   Let him go.

Dan.   He won't go far. He's been like this before,
       He's a moody cuss.

Hart.   Never as bad as this.

Ned (in gloomy anger).   He can go to hell.

Dan.   He doesn't mean it, Ned.
       He'll be back in half an hour; or he'll go on the grog
       And be back in the morning grinning as if nothing had
           happened.

Ned.   Something has happened.

Hart.   He's off. Listen!
       Full gallop down the gully. He'll break his neck.

                                                        (171–72)

Some of the themes of *The Fire on the Snow* are continued
in *Ned Kelly*. Courage is still to be valued, but in this case
it is reckless courage akin to bravado. Kelly is given a heroic
voice even if he is not given Scott's heroic stature. Australians
who revere the traditions of their "outback" have always
admired the daredevil—to "take a chance" is part of the bushman's creed. When the clergyman Gribble asks Kelly why he
rides "always the very brink of disaster," Kelly replies:

There's a thrill in it, parson: you wouldn't understand
Galloping like a landslide down a mountain,
Or lifting a horse and tearing away through the night
With dogs and guns and the squatter all bawling blue murder,
And the sounds growing fainter and farther away as you gallop.
Till you stop for a breather and listen, and hear
Nothing at all except your own mare blowing.

You've lost them again! And there's only the bush around you,
Your own dark bush that you know like the back of your hand.

(136–37)

It is this reckless daring that wins Kelly the uneasy, sometimes reluctant loyalty of his subordinates: Stewart developing
the theme of leadership makes this contrast with the "mind and
will" domination of Scott over his men. Stewart is examining,
in a sense, an Australian way of life; he is reminding us that
Australian values of leadership have tended to be equated with
physical rather than mental prowess.

We see this in the passage where Hart and Byrne, sitting in
their lonely hut in the mountains, decide, in Byrne's words,
that "a gang must have a leader."

Hart.   Joe, supposing something happened to Ned?

Byrne. We'd all be sunk.

Hart.   You're the brains of the outfit.

Byrne. But Ned's the heart. He's only got to laugh
        And we'll laugh till our ribs rattle; he's only to frown
        And we all sneak off and scowl the bark from the gum-trees.
        If he gives us the word for a raid———

Hart.   We'll do it as usual:
        Go for the traps for Ned,
        Fight for him, fall for him, swing for him, rot for
            Ned Kelly!

(160)

I suspect that Stewart is quietly making the point that the
man of action is the blood brother of the artist; his abundance
of primitive energy is just as necessary as the imagination of
the artist to put a civilized concept of life into creative action.
But the artist, the poet, cannot be subordinated, and for this
reason Sewart contrives to ensure that Kelly does not dominate
the play or our interest; Joe Byrne is the first of the bushrangers to appear on stage and it is he who captures our imagi-
nations and if the truth is told, our hearts, as Stewart fashions
him as poet, lover, wit, and philosopher, with his Irish charm

always to the fore. At the Jerilderie bank he waggishly christens
Living, one of the rather solemn clerks, "Inkpot":

> Living (with faint dignity). My name is Living.
>
> Byrne (cheerfully). Well, Living, you'll soon be dead.
>
> (109)

There is this feyness, too, in Byrne: Later on he says to Living:

> Some pay-day, Inkpot,
> I'm coming to stick you up for the whole of your screw.
> I'll raid your house. I'll steal your cuckoo clock,
> The one with your grandfather's knobs on. I'll burn your slippers,
> I'll pinch the family album, I'll tread on the garden,
> I'll chase your wife till she flies to the roof and squawks.
>
> (120)

He flirts with the barmaids in the hotels, jokes irreverently with
the clergyman Gribble ("Don't you dare save my soul. It
wouldn't agree wth me.") and boasts of his freedom from the
straitjacket of everyday life, regarding it as the grace of God
that he is not a clerk like Inkpot, "stiffened in the lines of a
ledger like a coffin," or like the Jerilderie schoolteacher, Elliott,
"hammering lessons through schoolboys' surly backsides."
Stewart keeps building the poetic content of Byrne's speeches,
and it is not the clergyman Gribble, with his dire threats of
"the first harsh gods of Australia, the lash and the gallows"
who underlines the inevitability of the gang's capture or death,
but Byrne's own poetic vision of the reckless folly that must
subsume tragedy:

> But so are we all mad.
> Why did we start on this? When things go wrong
> I live in a nightmare, the solid world dissolves:
> My hand, my fingers, this chair, this table, the hut,
> Nothing is real; everything slips into shadow,
> And the shadows are full of knives.
>
> (161)

Stewart admits that Byrne "took charge of the play; there's no doubt about that, but he was never intended to. There was actually a fair bit of idealism of myself in Byrne. Making him Irish gave a freedom to his language."[24] If the central motive of the play is the conflict of moral values between tamed man and lawless man, between the terrorized citizens and the Kelly gang itself, then it is surely Byrne who with humor and poetry alleviates the starkness of the contrast.

The Australian critic Arthur Phillips has offered the view that Stewart chose Byrne as the main voice in expressing the romantic or Ulyssean revolt against Telemachan respectability (represented in the play by the bank clerk Living, the schoolteacher Curnow, and others). Phillips develops his theory as follows:

The main theme of Stewart's play—though not its only one—is a study of the conflict of the Telemachan and the Ulyssean attitude. It is not merely a protesting assertion of the romantic revolt, or a complaint of that revolt's inevitable defeat. It is rather a study of the tragic conflict inherent in the theme, looking objectively at the subject, and loading no dice to satisfy a prejudice—although it is clear that Stewart's own sympathies lean towards the Ulyssean view of life. The play is not a justification of the Kellys—that a good many readers should have so misunderstood it is a significant illustration of our uneasy shame in the presence of the Kelly legend. Stewart's aim is rather to see the Kellys in the illuminating focus of imaginative creation, to explain them, and to relate them to the spiritual impulsions of their period and their country.[25]

Stewart took an Australian background for this, his second play; shrewdly aware of national attitudes and stances he was able here to put them in a form (rather than in, say, a contemporary social play) which would have as direct an appeal to future generations as to his own. Byrne says that he feels Australia burning in his mind "like a gun barrel"; the play in fact reflects many facets of the Australian character, as well as the Australian scene. Kelly rails at the fact that he, "a white Australian," is "hunted by blacks"; the railway workers at Glenrowan forced at gunpoint to rip up the tracks, shrug their shoulders:

we laid the rails for the government,
We'll root them up for the Kellys. It's all the same.

(197)

Australia is a tough country, is what Stewart is saying, and out
of its raw earth, its resistance to cultivation and civilization,
grew the Kellys and men like them. Haunted by the ghosts of
their past

("You would see," says Byrne,
. . . when you saw the Kellys, ghosts behind them,
Ghosts in chains, ghosts being whipped, hanged,
Ghosts in the mirror of every man's mind in Australia").

(212)

it was their destiny to hunt and be hunted, to kill and be killed.
Gribble, in a sense the Chorus of the play, hammers home the
realization that Stewart, I think, would have us all come to:

Australia's the violent country, the earth itself
Suffers, cries out in anger against the sunlight
From the cracked lips of the plains; and with the land,
With the snake that strikes from the dust,
The people suffer and cry their anger and kill.
I have come to understand it in love and pity;
Not horror now; I understand the Kellys.

(141)

We understand Kelly, then—the heroic will perverted, but still
the bush larrikin become folk hero; equated in the Australian
consciousness of men against odds even with Robert Scott
(whether that is just or not); given his fitting epitaph in words
of unaccustomed poetry by one of the police troopers who
shoots him down:

The mad, lonely life, and the lonely ending,
One man against all the world in the bush at Glenrowan.

(223)

H. G. Kippax, a leading Australian drama critic, has fittingly
summarized Stewart's achievement with this play:

Here all the birds in the bush of the "Australianist" legend came
home to roost—the underdog and his fight against society; the am-
biguous rebel seen as lawless hero; the collision between the capitalist
enterprise of the cities, and its conformist compulsions, and the
private enterprise of the bush; the epic themes of endurance and
of wandering in vast, hostile landscapes. And for the first time an
Australian playwright rose to them. . . .[26]

B. *The Golden Lover*

The Australian Broadcasting Commission, enthusiastic at the
success of *The Fire on the Snow*, conducted a nationwide competition for radio verse plays in 1942 which Stewart easily won with
The Golden Lover, first performed in 1943. While it would be
better judged in a radio version, even in printed form I find it
the most lyrically and emotionally satisfying of all Stewart's
plays. It is interesting to note that it is Stewart's favorite
play (but not his "best"—which honor he accords *Shipwreck*); he
has said to me in discussing it, "I think it's got more poetry and
more laughter than any of the others; it's more natural to myself.
And actually I loved writing it—which I usually don't."[27]

For the material of this play Stewart left strong heroic themes
and went back to his native New Zealand and its indigenous
people, the Maoris, with their myths and legends. It was an exercise more of nostalgia than of patriotism. He had grown up with
the customs and traditions of the Maoris well embedded in his
consciousness. The Taranaki episode of the Maori Wars had been
fought where he went to school; Maori children had been his
friends at school; he moved among Maoris when he was a young
newspaper reporter; he had visited their homes and stayed with
them when he was tramping around north of Auckland on holidays. Much of the feeling he got from these experiences went
into the play. He was reading James Cowan's *Faery Folk Tales
of the Maori* for an account of the story of Hinemoah and Tutanaki
—a very well known Maori legend in the Hero and Leander vein—
when he came across the legend of the Golden Lover and, as he
says, it hit him like a "blinding light."[28]

It is a romantic comedy in fantasy form about the beautiful
young Maori girl-wife Tawhai who is enchanted by Whana, the
chief of the light-skinned "patu paiarehe," meaning "people of

the mist," the fairies of Maori legend. (It is said that a wild forest tribe of Maoris with fair skins and red hair once existed, and that even now there are Maoris who have light complexions and auburn hair and who claim kinship with this earlier tribe). After several secret trysts with her golden lover, Tawhai, under the spell of her love for Whana, tries to strike a bargain with her husband (Ruarangi), father (Nukuroa), and mother (Wera) that she should spend her nights with her lover in the mists of the forest and her days in the village with her husband and family. In the end common sense or the pull of convention or latent kinship for her own people (certainly not affection for her fat, foolish, and lazy husband) triumphs and she reluctantly returns to her normal life. (There is of course the consolation of a young and virile lover, Tiki—for clearly Tawhai is not much better than she should be.) It is a story told with wit and a full appreciation of the droll and often waggish humor of the Maoris, and with Stewart in absolute command of his verse medium.

Clearly, Stewart here exploits once again but in much lighter vein, of course, the theme of the dream and the reality, the forbidden fruit of abandoned love and the cold realization of the obligations of domestic life in the family "whare," or hut. At the same time, as the Australian academic and critic Professor Harold Oliver has observed,[29] the listener or reader "may find in the story, if he pleases, a development through symbols of the theme that the perfect lover is merely the creation of the romantic mind":

You have dreamed about me. All your life you have dreamed.
I know you, Tawhai. You have had lovers, a husband,
And lovers and a husband they were not to be despised;
But always beyond them, Tawhai, there was a dream.
You lay, I know you have lain, with your lover in the bracken,
You have lain with your husband in the bed of fern in the whare,
But who did you lie with in dreams? With your golden lover!
With a tall man like a shadow on the fringe of the morning
Who turned and was gone before you could ask his name.
With a golden man who vanished in the green of the bush
Before you could see his face. Look in my eyes!
The golden lover haunting the fringe of your dreams. . . .

                                                        (61)

If Stewart had critics for his neglect of the women in the Ned Kelly story (Kelly's mother and sister play a prominent part in the saga but were not included in the verse drama) he more than made up for this in what is a study of extraordinary insight of the mind of a fickle, discontented and by inference sexually deprived, attractive young Maori woman. By turns petulant and generous, prim yet passionate, Tawhai is a 1942 prototype for "women's lib." When one of the old Maroi women suggests she anoint herself with shark oil, which is the legendary repellent for the fairy people, one can see Tawhai tossing her pretty head as she replies:

> Ruarangi, I do not wish to hear about shark oil.
> I am not a shoal of fish. I am a woman.
>
> (38)

Stewart's turn of poetic phrase consistently delights, as he limns this wayward girl, with her caprices and illogicalities. When she is told that her husband's jealousy of the young man Tiki may not be ill-founded, how nearly perfect is her womanly reply:

> If I have been slightly unfaithful from time to time
> It is most unjust to beat me on mere suspicion.
>
> (47)

Her amused contempt for her idle husband—"He is pleasant for a husband, a kind of walking joke"—and her capacity to play him like a fish on a rod, are never better illustrated than in an extraordinary passage wherein the astonishing flexibility of Stewart's verse-form has full play, in which tongue-in-cheek she baits her husband with her hopeless and spellbound love for Whana:

Tawhai.   Ruarangi, I am truly sorry. But what can I do?
          If only my will were not as water before him—

Ruarangi. If you say that again I will hit you hard on the head.

Tawhai.   But I am as water. I have never been bewitched like this
          In all my life. I simply cannot resist him.
          All that is happening is against my will as you know,
          But I cannot help consenting to its happening.

Ruarangi.   Ach, that disgusting beast, that monster of the mist,
              How dare he lay his hands on my wife's person!
              It is an outrage, Tawhai.

Tawhai.   It is shocking indeed.
              Although, Ruarangi, it is not completely revolting.
              Whana is strangely handsome.

Ruarangi.   He is a devil.

Tawhai.   I think it is hardly fair to call him a devil.
              He is, of course, of the patu paiarehe,
              But they, after all, though shameless in bewitching women,
              Are human enough in their way.

Ruarangi.   He is a dog.

Tawhai.   Oh, no! You must not say such a thing, Ruarangi.
              It is true he is not polite to bewitch me like this,
              But that is just his nature. We must not blame him.

Ruarangi.   I am going to Te Kawau to have you unbewitched.

Tawhai.   It is best to leave well alone.

Ruarangi.   It is not well!
              I will not have my wife coming home in the morning
              From nights in the vile clutches of that beast of the
                  mountains.

Tawhai.   Ah, he is not so vile. I wish you could meet him
              And see how nice he can be. I am sure you would like him.
              You would get on well together.

Ruarangi.   Tawhai, hear me!
              I will not meet him and I would not get on well
              With a red-haired devil of the forest who has stolen my
                  wife.
              You are shameless even to suggest it.

Tawhai.   How cruel you are.
              I am only trying to do what is best for you both.
              You are jealous, that is the trouble.

                                                              (79)

        Tawhai is real, a woman; Whana, her golden lover, a shadowy
figure, hardly emerging from the mists. The play movingly,

despite its basic humor, tells the love story of these two protagonists—a love story that cannot have a happy ending, because the dream cannot be the reality. And yet with great artistry Stewart contrives that the real woman is seen as the dreamer and the shadowy, fairy lover as the one who constantly poses the problems of reality. The loveliest verse in the play is contained in the lyricism of Whana's rapturous joy in his love in such passages as

> Lovely beyond all that is lovely in the earth or the sky
> And coming so to my feet! Beautiful, Tawhai,
> Is the silver Waipa, but the water runs from our fingers;
> Beautiful is the rimu-tree, the green-haired dreamer,
> But her eyes are blind and her feet are fastened in the earth;
> Beautiful is the blue sky and the sky of stars,
> Beautiful the white clematis and the wild white heron,
> But sky and flowers and water and tree and bird,
> They will not come to the hand. And you, you are here!
>
> (77)

and

> When the tui sings,
> The bell through the green of the forest, clear and deep,
> Some form arises trembling among the music
> Like a silver ghost, my darling. You are that ghost.
> When the kowhai breaks into flower and the honied blossoms
> Flow down to the earth in a waterfall still and silent,
> Some form that is not a tree laughs there and sings
> And bathes her hair and her hands in the golden pool:
> Your hair and your hands, you heart of the spring and its flowers.
> A green spirit in the forest, a dark in the earth,
> A fire of silver burning now with the stars—
> Tawhai, Tawhai, you are all the earth and the heavens.
>
> (63)

And yet these impassioned feelings give way eventually to his demand that he should face her family and friends, and the old witchdoctor Te Kawau, who is called in to break the golden lover's spell.

> Look in the furthest shadows to the whare where you lived
> And the little village you loved.
>
>   (97)

Whana tells her, and so loses her. In the final scene of this play
of seven scenes the dramatic intensity, the pure poetry of
emotions strung as fine as fiddlestrings, constitutes a piece of
writing which Stewart has not bettered. He sets the stage with
verbal magic: the village, the audience of villagers, and the
principal players—father, mother, the husband, the love-torn
Tawhai now fluttering like a frightened bird, the godlike Whana
("Did you see him leap from the shadows?" says an awed
villager), confronted by his implacable adversary, the old witchdoctor Te Kawau. Eventually it is the voice of Te Kawau, become
a poet too, that becomes the relentless hammer shattering the
bowl of dreams to fragments:

> Tawhai . . .
> . . . no fire burns for ever.
> Now dream no more, you who are woman awake.
> Know you are woman. Not a flower of the forest nor a fire
> But a woman of the Maori here among your people.
> The golden lover—what is that but the god of a dream?—
> A dream that will break as the day breaks on Pirongia.
> You know, and he knows too, it is only a dream,
> A love like another love, the dream of a night
> To fade with the dawn, turn ugly or nothing in a year,
> Or die at the best to the little embers of laughter.
>
>   (99)

In the agony of Tawhai's threnody we see her clutching the
fragments of reality to her heart:

> You are wise, Te Kawau,
> But never will I forget this man of the mist
> Who struck at my heart like a golden hawk from the sky.
>
>   (100)

Perhaps, too, Stewart means his story to be taken as an allegory
of woman's desire to have simultaneously the perfect romance

of free and unfettered love and yet the comfortable stability of married life, or for that matter every human being's paradoxical yearning for the romantically strange and at the same time for the reassuringly familiar. But all this too is only a variant of Stewart's favorite preoccupation with the impossible dream measured against the reality of everyday life.

The play, however, can be enjoyed for much more than its main themes. Stewart has caught in tone, image, and rhythm not only the beauty and grandeur of New Zealand's mountains, forests, and rivers, but the tribal traditions and the folklore of the people themselves as expressed in the natural poetry of their conversations. And shot through all this is humor: it is not only that despite the tender and romantic love story he tells, Stewart intended the play as a piece of comedy (he says he wrote it with great enjoyment, "sitting alone in [his] flat at Kings Cross rocking with laughter at [his] own jokes"[30]), but the charm of the play lies in the droll and gently satirical fun of the Maoris going about their daily lives. We see this expressed in so many ways: in Tawhai's domestic exchanges with Ruarangi,

> Ruarangi: I, too, shall work
> A warrior's work, I shall sit out here in the sun
> At the side of the whare, and look at my fishing lines.
>
> Tawhai: You must not exhaust yourself.
>
> (37)

in the artless litotes of Ruarangi's threat,

> Should you happen to go for a walk with that young Tiki,
> I think he will take a longer walk one day
> With a split skull, and he will not come back.
>
> (37)

in old Wera's timeless sapience, with such observations as,

> All men are fools
> Though I do not think a whare is a whare without one.
>
> (47)

and,

                           It does no good
                To ask where a woman has gone when a woman has gone
                Wherever a woman goes when she goes for a walk.

                                                        (56)

All this Stewart has clearly enjoyed in his writing, as he has in
using this picturesqueness of phrase of the Maori for what is
essential to the radio dramatist's craft—the conveying of description in truly dramatic comment, or better still, in dialogue with
the sparse vividness of his poetry. There is no better example
of this than the description of the witchdoctor Te Kawau
through the words of Tawhai:

                He is old and yellow and evil and feeds on horror
                Like fungus on a rotten log.

                                                        (36)

    Leslie Rees has remarked[31] on the parallel in theme and
atmosphere to this play of Yeat's *The Land of Heart's Desire*,
in that occasionally Stewart's play catches a similar accent and
rhythm. When the fairy lover of the mist, with his burning
hair, makes his promise to Tawhai of

                The fire that leaps from the darkness and never grows cold,
                The flower that blooms in the forest and never grows old,
                The hands that are never coarsened, the body of dawn
                That never is gross with day or haggard with dusk—

                                                        (63)

it is true we are reminded of Yeats's land,

                Where nobody gets old and godly and grave,
                Where nobody gets old and crafty and wise,
                Where nobody gets old and bitter of tongue.

But whereas Yeats's play is essentially and sparely mystical
Stewart's is ultimately a domestic comedy, with a romantic, even
fairy, theme never allowed to escape from the matter-of-fact
confines of an eternal triangle plot set in a parochial and interlocking community. Common to both is the quality of poetry

which in each case lifts it into the realm of literary delight, and in the case of Stewart's play makes it something of lasting fascination.

D. *The Earthquake Shakes the Land*

Inspired no doubt by the success of *The Golden Lover* Douglas Stewart wrote a second play on a New Zealand–Maori theme, *The Earthquake Shakes the Land*. It was performed by the ABC in 1946. I have not heard it on the air, but according to Leslie Rees, who was the ABC's Assistant Director of Drama at the time, it was "only a half success."[32]

Judging by the script one can see the reason for this. The main theme, or rather the general background of the play, is the Maori Wars of the 1840s. Crisscrossing are a number of subsidiary themes or subplots: the smoldering resentment of Maoris against white settlers who, they claimed, had filched their lands; the contrasting ideologies of the Maoris themselves between those agitating for uprising and war and those seeking peace; the efforts of a subject people to retain or even redeem its dignity; the tangled complications of a mixed marriage; and the relationships between two sets of marriage partners. Stewart tried to accomplish all this as verse-drama within the space of an hour-long script, and to embrace in its final action warfare between opposing armies as well. It is much too ambitious and hence too confusing, and Stewart has admitted as much: "I've never cared very much for it; the Maoris are a bit statuesque in it, I think; it was a conscientious attempt to analyse war which is too big a subject anyhow—it's all a bit too self-conscious."[33]

The protagonists are MacDonald, a Scottish farmer living with a Maori girl, Ngaere, by whom he has a child, and Kimo, a minor Maori chief and his wife, Ata (Ngaere's sister). War is in the air; rival Maori leaders are urging war and peace; Kimo, whose superficial friendship for MacDonald conceals a resentment developing into hatred of him, as a representative of the pakeha (i.e., white man) who has stolen Maori land, throws in his lot with the Maori leader, Rewi, the leader of the Maori faction urging war against the white settlers and the government. MacDonald, stubborn, addicted to drink, and blind to his danger, offers to trade his wife and child to the Maoris if he can keep his land; this action drives Ngaere into the arms of Kimo, for whom she has long nourished a passion. She goes off to war with Kimo, who also renounces Ata. Ata favors the course of peace rather than war, is sympathetic to MacDonald and his desire to farm his land unmolested, and thus has to endure the scorn of her sister and unfaithful husband, as well as of her people. Ngaere's hatred for MacDonald grows to match Kimo's; indeed, she persuades Kimo to kill MacDonald as the first act of war. In the war scenes that follow, Rewi is killed, the Maoris are defeated by the government soldiers, and Ngaere is left lonely and lamenting. The play is constructed of eleven scenes.

As I have said, it is the sheer complication of it all that defeats Stewart, yet there are aspects of the play's development and its writing that equal the best work in his previous plays. Characterization, for instance, is much more clearly defined. MacDonald, when one considers the difficulties of the verse medium for this, remains starkly in the memory. In a number of passages of forceful writing Stewart makes a convincing and indeed sympathetic character out of this dour, stubborn Scot:

> I'll never go.
> I made this farm. Made it with my hands and my sweat.
> I've sunk my life in it. I've grown a part of myself
> In every pine and every fruit-tree I've planted.
> I've ploughed a part of myself into the ground
> Whenever I've turned a furrow. My blood's in the grass.
> The wheat grows out of my body. Would I leave all that
> Because a few savages dance a dance in the night?

His solace is not Ngaere—who is to him merely a chattel—but his land and his whiskey, and Stewart puts into his mouth a quotation for all seasons:

> But the world's harsh
> And the whisky makes it kinder.

He has no love, rather contempt, for his half-caste child:

> There's a village in the Highlands, away across the ocean,
> Where generations of hard, God-fearing MacDonalds,

Presbyterians forebye with huge red granite tombstones
Would rise and thunder to the Lord to see this sight,
Old whiskered pious ghosts, raging in the kirkyard.
My Maori baby! My piccaninny!

But it is in the device of the soliloquy that Stewart most powerfully projects MacDonald into the minds of his listeners and indeed considers this to be the best piece of writing in the play.[34] In sixty-odd lines he takes us deep into MacDonald's consciousness, as, bereft, in utter loneliness, and surrounded by his enemies, he drinks with and soliloquizes to his shadow:

Night. And a man alone. And the times bad.
A lamp and a bottle and a shadow. Shadow, my lad,
Will you have a drink with me, Shadow?

His Calvinist soul revolts at his "sin"—he comes back time and time again to his soul's ulcer:

What have I done with my life
But lived with a Maori wench, begotten a half-caste.
My son's no son to me, nor ever could be.
I've joked about it, called him the brown MacDonald,
The wee Scots thistle sown in a foreign pasture.
I've made it a joke. A joke? There have been nights
I sat up drinking alone and laughed about it,
And shook in my soul at my laughter. Now if I laugh,
I laugh like you, Shadow. I open my mouth,
Grin on the wall, but never a sound comes out.

It is a brilliant portrayal in poetry of a man in agony of spirit, facing the loss of the only thing left for him to love—his land—which, as we come to see, is more important to him than his life.

Scarcely less impressive is Stewart's translation of Ngaere from the submissive woman dominated by MacDonald to the bloodthirsty Lady Macbeth, who screws Kimo's courage to the sticking place:

I watched the struggle of his body. I am watching now
The dark pool that is spreading over the grass;
It flows in my mind and my body, I am warm all over.

Paradoxically, in a play which, in the estimation of author, critics, and audiences was his least successful, Stewart has answered (in some aspects of it, at least) what he wrote of once as the prime challenge to the verse playwright—that "poetic drama must try the most daring thing and surrender any momentary advantage that may be got from making up with nice poetry what is lacking in dramatic quality..." and that "every individual on earth speaks in a different rhythm and that theoretically there are as many kinds of poetic rhythm to be used as there are men and women...."[35]

No better illustration of these principles, and nothing more dramatically powerful in Stewart's verse exists than in the scene where Kimo, with the cry and clash of war in the background, and the atmosphere brooding and tense with evil and passion, first of all rouses Ngaere to respond to his desire for her, using the tensions of war and patriotism to fire her:

Ngaere: ...I heard them, Kimo,
         The cry of the warriors in the sunlight, down by the river.
         And it sounded like my own heart beating. Storm, storm,
         The sound of storm in the land. We grow tired of summer,
         The long grass and the sleepy water and the bellbirds,
         Weeds in the channel where the current sang like a man.
         Something I needed in my blood, the beat of the storm;
         I heard my own heart beating, just for a moment.
         But it died, it died, it died.

Kimo: Listen, Ngaere!

Chorus: (DISTANT)
         Red, red, red the wing of the bird;
         Bird in the green bush and his wing is red.

Ngaere: The man at the pa!

Kimo: I told you the river was flowing.

Ngaere: But where is it taking them, Kimo? Where are we going?

Kimo: Ngaere, how can I know? I tell you I don't
         Care where it takes us, Ngaere. It is taking me
         To you, that is all I care about.

Ngaere: Kimo,
         It is all too late.

Kimo: Too late? You are beautiful, Ngaere.
          Like a night of storm yourself, so tall and dark
          And clashing with the forces of destruction. When they
                    shout down there
          They shout for you. You who left the Maoris
          And gave so much, gave yourself to the pakeha:
          So much, so much, because you despised your people.
          Come back, they say. You lost glory of our people,
          You spirit of our people, dark and fierce and beautiful,
          A storm in the land, come back to the life of the Maori.
          And when you hear the people shouting that song,
          They have one voice; it is mine, I want you, Ngaere.

and then takes her as she wildly clings to the image of MacDonald
at the moment of her submission:

Ngaere: No, it is wrong.

Kimo: What do you care if it is?
          I know you, you want the darkness. A Maori lover
          Who knows what you feel when the tribes are shouting
                    for war
          And your blood shouts in your ears. You are big and tall,
          Your hair is leaves at midnight, your mouth proud,
          A light hides in your eyes like a killing in the night
          And now the times are tall and the sky all black,
          The tribes are coming from north and south for the killing
          And you with your proud mouth, a chief's daughter,
          Are the wild heart of it all. The war is coming
          And you are the war-dance. Your feet stamp in my brain.
          Ngaere—

Ngaere: You are huge, you are like a darkness round me,
          You smother me with evil and terror.

Kimo: If it is that,
          Let it be that. We are not afraid of evil.
          Everything is evil now if you call it evil
          When the hidden rivers break out and race in the night.
          We are the rivers, we are the waves of the earthquake,
          We are the nation and we rush together to our fate,
          No one can stand in our way.

Ngaere: You are MacDonald.

> This is MacDonald's hand, MacDonald's mouth.
> O, MacDonald, MacDonald my love. Hold me, MacDonald.

Kimo: I will kill you for this.

Ngaere: Kill me, choke me, Kimo.

When Ngaere, "all passion spent," speaks the last line of the play;
her lover dead, her people overthrown, sans child and family,
and her life now a shell, the words—empty and anticlimactical—
are artistically perfect.

> I am a dead woman on the hill of the dead.

E. *Shipwreck*

This play is written around the mutiny and massacre which
resulted when the Dutch navigator Pelsart's ship *Batavia* was
wrecked on the northwest coast of Australia, in 1629. The story
unfolds in three acts and seven scenes, with one setting—"the
interior of a large tent of the marquee type where boxes, chests,
wine kegs, oars, ropes and other litter that might have been
salvaged from a wrecked ship are piled or strewn in confusion."[36]
Pelsart sails off in an open boat some 2,000 miles north for Java
to get help, leaving Cornelius, the super-cargo, in command. The
chief characters among those left behind are the loyal Corporal
Hays, who sets off with a party of twenty men to a neighboring
island to look for water; van Mylen, a merchant, and his wife,
Lucretia; Sebastian, a minister, and his daughter, Judith, who
are voyaging in the *Batavia*, along with Heynorick, Commodore
Pelsart's devoted butler, and van Apeldoorn, the ship's officer.
Two of the complement of soldiers, Huyssen and Seevanck, take
a prominent part in the action; there is also a party of women
aboard, wives of artisans, four of whom have speaking parts.

Cornelius, attracted by the treasure retrieved from the wreck,
a lust for power and for Lucretia, leads a mutiny with Huyssen
and Seevanck as his right-hand men, cuts down the loyal soldiers,
and murders van Mylen and the artisans. The wives of the latter
are divided among the men; Huyssen takes Judith (who goes not
unwillingly); Cornelius rapes and takes Lucretia. Sebastian,
weak and negative as a character, is eventually goaded into

killing Huyssen and is then himself killed by Seevanck. The mutineers then plan to make a surprise attack on the loyal Hays and his men, but the gentle and servile Heynorick, at Lucretia's promptings, rows out at night and warns Hays of the attack. The mutineers are ambushed and killed, with the exception of Seevanck, who is captured, and Cornelius who, wounded, escapes back to the main camp. In the midst of this confusion, Pelsart returns, and in the final scene, dies suddenly while meting out summary justice to Seevanck and Cornelius (both to have their hands lopped, and to be hung and left on the gibbet as a warning to other mutineers). The survivors then sail back to Holland.

It should be said at once that *Shipwreck* is regarded by most Australian literary critics as the least successful of Stewart's four major plays. James McAuley does not see in it "the same density of interest as *Ned Kelly*"; the play, he feels, "seems to have been overmastered by the raw potential of its 'colorful' theme";[37] J. F. Burrows writes that "unfortunately the play as a whole does not live up to its protagonist. . . . The comparative failure of *Shipwreck* is the more unfortunate because in that play Stewart's ideas take on the universality of *The Fire on the Snow*, the harshness of *Ned Kelly* and the symbolic force and discipline of *The Golden Lover*."[38] Nancy Keesing, who has written a major critical assessment of Stewart's work, believes that "as a play, the work is unbalanced by evil men."[39] David Bradley writes of its "moral repulsiveness."[40] Leslie Rees, Australia's foremost drama critic and mentor of Stewart's radio-play career, follows up Nancy Keesing's criticism more forthrightly; he considers it to be a disappointing play—one of "tempestuous vigor rather than of true power." He continues:". . . the main challenge is this. How are we to assess a drama soaked for almost its total length in blood and rape? Has not the author's theory of the value of extreme violence as a fertilizer of poetic and artistic fulfillment perhaps trapped him into a harshness of mind out of harmony with the elementary spiritual purity of great works?"[41] (It should be noted, too, that the play has not enjoyed much success when staged in Australia—and that, as Stewart somewhat ironically recalls, "the ABC banned *Shipwreck*, it was considered naughty."[42])

Now, this reaction is the more surprising against Stewart's own opinion that *Shipwreck* is the best of his plays—"the best constructed and the deepest and the most powerful."[43] This assessment, I feel, must be examined against Stewart's own philosophy of the themes and purpose of poetic drama. First of all he has always believed that it is chiefly the difficulty of discovering and telling the full truth about the events of a writer's time that sends the poetic dramatist to historical themes. He has been consistent about this, setting all his dramas against events in history (or legend). In the case of *Shipwreck,* I believe his concern with violence and its manifestations of murder, rape, and avarice mirrored his apprehensions about the state of contemporary society—a view that in the 1970s he must surely see as vindicated, not only in the behavior of contemporary society, but in the very themes of plays, films, and novels with which presentday writers have become so involved, if not obsessed. (In any case, as Nancy Keesing notes,[44] Stewart told her he regarded *Shipwreck* as a means of expressing the wartime struggles of the Australian Army against Japan—suggesting an analogy, for instance, between the castaways and their predicament, and the Australian prisoners of war in the Changi prison camp, who had no escape from the bestial cruelties of their guards.) The capacity of men to behave as beasts, or indeed of natural forces to assume bestial guises, has been a preoccupation of Stewart throughout his plays. Oates's body became the prey of "the beaks and talons of the blizzard"; Ned Kelly was "the dingo at the throats of the sheep," his gang "beasts in their lairs." Cornelius, in *Shipwreck,* is variously described as an ape, a weevil, a "red bull—with his horns dripping with blood." Cornelius himself, when told that his men have carried off and raped Rose Harman, the wife of the murdered carpenter, comments sardonically, "When you keep lions, they have to be fed like lions." Lucretia encapsulates the concept when she describes the mutineers as men who have "all gone wild. Back to the beasts of the jungle."

Second, Stewart has consistently refused to accept anything less than heroic themes or human emotions brought to a pitch where bloodshed and catharsis follow inevitably, as the forces best capable of nourishing genuine poetic drama. In other words, he subscribes to the Greek tradition. It is for this reason that while he yields to none in his admiration of Eliot's *Murder in the Cathedral* ("the poetry of humanity,"[45] he once called it), he has no use for what he regards as the banalities of theme and dialogue of Eliot's other plays.

But when the conversation is restricted, as it is largely in *The Confidential Clerk*—and as it was to a slightly lesser extent in *The Family Reunion* and *The Cocktail Party*—to the kind of chitchat that passes at afternoon tea, a language without any of the significance of activity, as far removed from any vital contact with the earth, as a currant bun is removed from a field of wheat—it just does not seem possible to achieve poetry.[46]

Now it can be argued, I suppose, that a lack of a feeling for reality, a feeling or understanding of what men and women actually do in the intervals between their heights of heroic passion or determined resolve, is necessary to bring a play closer to life. Certainly the lack of this can be argued in *The Fire on the Snow* where, from beginning to end, it is desperate trial and suffering; and *Shipwreck*, where Pelion of bloodlust seems to be piled on to Ossa of crisis (though less true of *Ned Kelly*, where we see the characters concerning themselves with the comparative trivia of everyday events in their periods of waiting). But Stewart, I think, has the answer to this view, too. He expressed the opinion, several years before he wrote *Shipwreck*, that any substantial literary work "must concern itself with a single central motive worked out by the conflict of personality and dramatized by a sequence of events forcing the motive to a final crisis."[47] There is no room in such a concept for the trivia of domestic living or the prattle of polite society. Nor is there room for the play of contemporary social manners. "In fiction," he wrote once, "we expect to read the truth about life: in a play we see such an image or distillation of the truth as may be confined in the box of the stage."[48] The observation is relevant, too, that *Shipwreck* in stage terms is more easily capable of production than *Ned Kelly* (its sister play in that it, too, was primarily written for the stage)—whereas the latter called for two separate pub scenes, a bank, two huts in the ranges, and a railway embankment, *Shipwreck* is confined to one set, though at that, with more lavish trappings of costume and incidentals.

Two themes of Stewart's earlier plays are predominant in *Shipwreck*—the impossible dream (of Cornelius) broken upon actuality and the implications of leadership, whether represented in the behavior and example of the leader himself (as in Robert Scott and Ned Kelly) or in the relationship, in this play, between the legitimate leader, Pelsart, and the mutineer-upstart Cornelius —a relationship which appears to put the question of the value of sheer vitality within a context of lawless violence.

Cornelius's dream is confused, ultimately spurious, and at best a metaphor for egoism. He contemplates his dream when he gloats over the hoard he has stolen, "two chests of treasures crammed," and tells Heynorick:

> . . . there are women in the world as white with beauty
> As the clearest diamond in my bedroom, and as red with passion,
> As the ruby that winks and chuckles and glares like a wolf.
>
> (245)

Huyssen, his more practical and cynical lieutenant-in-crime, acts in some way as the chorus to convince Cornelius of the futility of his dream, likening him to a fairy-tale king surrounded by every trapping of hedonism:

> You sit here and look at the jewels,
> You go into your bedroom and gloat over all the gold
> And you try to pretend it's yours. You're living in a dream
> You think you're lying on silk in your marble palace
> With somebody's wife—van Mylen's, eh, Cornelius?
> But you're not. It's not a palace here, but an island;
> It's Pelsart's money; and you'll never have your Lucretia.
>
> (246)

But in the end it is Cornelius himself who rejects his own dream, in his final confrontation with Pelsart:

> . . . you left me on this island
> With a woman like a moon in harvest—I'd dreamed about her—

And a fortune in gold and jewels to be had for the taking,
And men to tempt me, and wine—made me drunk and mad.

Pelsart. That was your own doing.

Cornelius.   Yours. You destroyed me.

(305)

Indeed, the characterization of Cornelius, as a multifaceted
villain, is one of Stewart's major literary triumphs. He has a kind
of black wit—"I am married myself—To a kind of old shoe, in
Holland. I left it behind"—manifested also in his idea, since there
are not enough women to go around, to make the men pay
them, so "they'll go home rich." Though he seizes power, his
caution and indecision yield him up to the dominance of his
coarser henchmen, Seevanck and Huyssen. He is a hand-washing
Pilate, unwilling to soil his "soft white hands—and yet simultaneously capable of mind-boggling sadism. But above all Stewart
has created in Cornelius an unforgettable picture of sheer evil,
almost unbearably exemplified in the terrible passage where
Cornelius presages his rape of Lucretia;

The lily and the frog,
You'd never have thought they'd have swum in the same pool.
Frog, he's humble; frog, he knows what he is;
Bullfrog; toad; drunk with the white of the lily;
That's why he lost his voice; can only croak.
I croak for you then, I hop for you then, Lucretia.
Come hop, come hop, must have you.

(Crouching and gesturing, and light on his feet
almost as if actually hopping, he moves towards her.)

(271)

Pelsart is not like Scott, or even Ned Kelly, represented as an
heroic leader in his brief appearances at the beginning and end
of the play; his indecision and instability are mirrored in his
physical weakness; "you think it looks like desertion?" he asks
van Mylen before he leaves for Java; and there are worlds of
irony in his statement that "Cornelius . . . has more authority than
I have. . . . He will enforce order. . . ." At the end his sentences

of hand-lopping before hanging have the vindictiveness of the weak man. And yet this matter of the lack of moral and spiritual, even of courageous, leadership is probably Stewart's thesis for demonstrating the unbridled violence that follows. It is Lucretia who cuts Cornelius down to size.

Cornelius.   Clothes for a king and jewels for a king and queen
              And who's the king of the island now Pelsart has gone?

Lucretia.   You're the king. You're a silly old King Nepture
              Who came up out of the sea. A king of the sea
              In a fairy tale that won't be true any more
              When Pelsart comes back to the island.

                                                        (243)

The chief interest in the play's characters centers upon the struggle between Cornelius and Lucretia: there is nothing in his erratic makeup than can subdue her pride and aloofness, and this is powerfully underlined in some lines of Stewart's best writing when she speaks her last words to him:

        No, I don't hate you, Cornelius. You can die in peace;
But die, but die, die! They'll leave you on the gallows
Like a tongue in the bell of the sky, the voice of this rock
Crying and clanging in a silent music of anguish
And if I were still on this island it might be a sweet
Or a harsh or a pitiful sound, but we sail at daybreak
And I'll never hear it. Not a whisper. I hope to foget you.

                                                     (303)

Characterization is another of Stewart's triumphs in this play—more than in his previous plays the characters are clear and distinct, even if most of them are unpleasant. I think Stewart is especially successful in his depiction of the butler Heynorick, a "little" man, who standing and waiting, as it were, performs the deed of astonishing bravery that brings the villains to book. Looking back on the plays we see that this careful illumination of the lives of the ordinary people—who are set in stark contrast against the brilliance or bravery or arrogance of their leaders—is another well-established theme used by Stewart—a typically

Australian concept, related perhaps to the idea of "mateship," and the alleged egalitarianism that characterizes Australian society. Byrne in *Ned Kelly* talks to Curnow, the insignificant Glenrowan schoolteacher (who warns the police train and thus like Heynorick performs the one deed of exceptional and unaccustomed courage which brings retribution and punishment to the wrongdoers)

> You know Curnow, I think of men like you
> Meek little men who'd never lift a horse
> Never lift a hand to a gun, never one moment
> Stand up on the sun and flower like a man into action.
> (208)

Ruarangi in *The Golden Lover* talks in the same strain:

> We are a little people and the bush surrounds us,
> A handful of warriors, a handful of women and children.
> (80)

So it is with Heynorick; he is one of the "little people"; the guise of servility conceals, as we see in one striking scene, a hatred of the mutineers and a love and loyalty for his Commodore, when he soliloquizes before a boar's head, reviling it and gesticulating in front of it with a drawn sword, as if it were the hated Cornelius. Eventually he carries out his act of bravery, and then lapses into his servitor's role, speaking the epitaph for Pelsart:

> He was a gentleman, sir. Too fine for the sea.
> (308)

Pastor Sebastian is a "little man" too: he invites pity and contempt for his fatuousness and for his moral cowardice when he does nothing to prevent the mutiny—even though he looks only to save his own and his daughter's life. He survives, in humiliation and terror, and then rises again in one of the great dramatic moments of the play when he kills Huyssen the mutineer, to whom his daughter has been given.

I do not like this play particularly, but this is mainly on the grounds of subject matter: I much prefer the charm and the magic of *The Golden Lover* and the stark but gripping realism of *The Fire on the Snow*. But I believe nevertheless that in *Shipwreck* Stewart reached his heights as a poetic dramatist, assured in the flexibility and narrative power of his verse, whether in conversation or description, displaying a precise sense of character against true light and shade, and demonstrating, above all, a final mastery in his understanding of the conflicts which beset human beings and the dreams with which they shield themselves.

It could hardly be expected that *Shipwreck* would fulfill the requirements of Matthew Arnold, who demanded majesty of subject, an "excellent action." Are a mutiny and massacre (or, for that matter, the depredations and killings of a band of outlaws) of sufficient dignity to justify a play's theme? Stewart believes so—considering that for his purposes, sufficient dignity can be created as was created from themes of the passions and deaths of princes (when princes were important) by his predecessors in ages past. There may not be the pomp and power of Caesar and Anthony in Pelsart and Cornelius, but there are, in Stewart's thinking, contemporary implications of warfare, suffering, and extremes of human behavior under stress and temptation, in the underlying universality of *Shipwreck*.

F. *Fisher's Ghost*

In his collection of essays in literary criticism, *The Flesh and the Spirit*, published in 1948 (most of the essays had been written prior to that date), Douglas Stewart in "The Meaning of Humour" quoted a statement by John Cowper Powys that "the true reality of life is the humour of life." Stewart continued with his own thoughts in this vein:

. . . comedy, though it may seem paradoxical to say so, has a spiritual significance. The purpose of humour is to reconcile man to life on this earth as a passing comedy in which he is not finally involved; to remind him that he might as well enjoy being a man while he has to be. . . . What better service can you do mankind than to make it laugh?

(p. 263)

Stewart still maintains this stance. He does not see it as the writer's job to depress people, "to keep on one long groan about the great fundamental truths which everybody knows anyhow—that you're going to grow old, you're going to die. I think you can do more people good by making them enjoy their life while they are here."[49]

This philosophy is especially well illustrated in *Fisher's Ghost* and particularly in the fact that, having dealt in his previous plays with themes involving the strongest human emotions—endurance, morality of behavior, passion and violence—he chose to make his last play a small jewel of humor, a romp into Australia's convict past, "a historical comedy," as, with tongue in cheek, he has subtitled it.

First published in 1960,* it is presented in an uninhibited mixture of colloquial prose and verse, carefully set against the speech usages of its time-setting of the 1820s in Australia. The ballad form takes precedence in the verse, and one is aware that Stewart was at this time occupied with his project of editing early Australian bush songs and ballads. He had noted with obvious regret, some years earlier, the decline of the Australian ballad form, pointing out that after its full flowering in the work of A. B. ("Banjo") Paterson,[50] Henry Lawson, and others in the 1890s, it had steadily grown unfashionable in the years up to the First World War, "when the ballad ceased to be the vehicle for vigorous storytelling and became largely a lament for the good old days."[51] Here then, I imagine, in *Fisher's Ghost* Stewart decided to make a lighthearted contribution toward redressing the balance. The play itself Stewart intended to be one of a set of light comedies trying to capture the spirit of Australian humor. The others, he says, "didn't come off."[52] The idea of *Fisher's Ghost* was to catch an Arcadian flavor by means of "whatever myths or fairies that we may have."[53]

The story of the play is based on a well-established legend of the Campbelltown district, a town on the southern outskirts of Sydney. A narrator sets the scene:

---

* Quotations from *Fisher's Ghost* that follow are taken from the edition published by the Wentworth Press (Sydney, 1960).

Here a song of Australia,
Now every year by year
The night that Fisher was murdered
Does Fisher's ghost appear.

He climbs out of that hole again,
No man knows why or how,
And sits upon that fence all night
As you may see him now.

(9)

The ghost ruminates about the identity of his murderer,

Oh who was it who did me in
And then concealed my body?
(11)

A policeman appears, and obligingly fills in the details. The ghost of Fisher finds out that his murderer was one George Worrall, his erstwhile partner, who having killed Fisher and buried the body claimed the title deeds of his small farm and sold some of the property. George Worrall comes on the scene and engages in guilt-ridden conversation with the ghost; a constable and native-tracker appear and are led to the "body" by the ghost. Worrall is arrested; we next see him hanged; and when he is become a ghost, and the two ghosts converse, we see that this is an annual event (both in fact being ghosts, since Worrall was actually hanged for the murder when it occurred), and one or the other of the ghosts "thinks it all up" each anniversary. The play ends with their mutual resolve:

The only thing that we can do
Is both of us stop haunting.
(41)

The play hardly bears literary analysis—it was never intended to be a vehicle for such an exercise. Stewart's somewhat irreverent attitude, even to the play as play, is marked by personal asides at odd points. For instance, a stage direction at the scene of Worrall's hanging, reads:

(The curtain lifts, and Worrall is seen hanging
from a limb of the gumtree in the centre of the stage.
Naturally, care should be taken of the actor in this
operation, if he is valuable. . . .)

(38)

Stewart's enjoyment of his freewheeling ballad form is obvious. The cheerful inconsequentialism of his rhyming

Nothing to do like all you useter
But sometimes hoot like a cold, wet rooster

(10)

is matched by the consistency and authenticity of his use of the
slang of the day—"cove" and "bloke" (for "person"); "dunny"
(for "lavatory"); "lags" (for "convicts"); and expressions like
"Fair dinkum," "By cripes," "Gawds truth"—which give color,
life, and raciness to the writing. There are such felicities of
versification as

Owls go swish and frogs go hoppity
Hooves at midnight clippetty-cloppitty,
Who was it stole Fred Fisher's property?

(19)

and occasionally Stewart, with more serious intent, touches the
authentic, traditional ballad note of his Scottish forbears as in
this eyewitness account of Fisher's murder:

I saw them there with a stick or an axe,
I saw them hit at something;
I cannot see in the dark and the fog
Oh what is that you are thumping?

Oh is it a man you are killing there,
Or a kangaroo for eating?
—It is a dog, said Billy Pike,
It is a dog we're beating.

Oh woe the deed and woe the night
That I should take his word;

It must have been Fred Fisher then
That they did thump so hard.

(24)

Here and there too Stewart writes in the lyric vein that is characteristic of so much of his general poetical output:

I saw the little clear brown pool
(Oh where is Fisher buried?)
Where water-bettles chase the sun
And dragonflies are married.

I saw the floating water-spinners
(What's that beneath the rocks?)
Whose shadows lie on the sand below
Like footfalls of a fox.

(34–35)

Keith Macartney has observed that "the poetry in this short dramatic excursion can be regarded as more consistently successful than the ambitious but uneven poetic dialogue of his full length plays."[54] Stewart's answer to that is that it is "going a bit far"; for his part "the poetry that's in it, the stuff that's any good is pastiche of old bush song and folk poetry." This, I think, places it correctly. *Fisher's Ghost* will find its chief value in the history of Australian literature as a conscious and successful attempt to crystallize something of the admittedly rather exiguous folklore of a comparatively new country into enduring form, distilling and catching in the process some elements of the Australian language, in much the same way as Synge did for the Irish.

IV   *Douglas Stewart's Place in Australian Drama*

Briefly, one must first look at Stewart's achievement in terms of the state of Australian drama in the 1940s. It would be safe to say that during that decade he was Australia's best known playwright, largely because of the wide audience captured throughout the country by the broadcasting of four of his plays. Many people who had never seen a play in their lives, much less a verse play, had their first taste of an Australian drama in one or another of these broadcast performances. Radio, of course (and television, for that matter), cannot take the place of stage performances, yet it is worth recalling that H. M. Green, doyen of Australia's literary historians, could write in 1961 of *Ned Kelly*: "there has been nothing so good, for the stage or radio, written in this country."[55]

However, the quite astonishing advance of Australian drama since World War II, the fillip given to local dramatic writing by the advent of television in 1956, and a belated but increasingly substantial patronage by government grants to theater and to creative dramatic writing, have changed the scene completely. From the international success of Ray Lawler's *The Summer of the Seventeenth Doll* to the emergence of modern playwrights also achieving overseas success such as David Williamson, Alex Buzo, and others, a wider and more sophisticated appreciation of drama has emerged. And no longer do we have that phenomenon—for such it was—of the 1940s that a *verse*-dramatist was probably the best-known playwright in Australia. But therein is Stewart's place in the history of Australian drama—that he to this day stands supreme among those who have essayed poetic drama, whether for stage or broadcasting.

CHAPTER 4

Douglas Stewart as Prose Writer

STEWART'S published creative prose is limited to his collection of short stories, A Girl with Red Hair (1944);* several
short stories published in The Bulletin after he had settled in
Australia, and a book of essays, The Seven Rivers (1966).* The
stories in A Girl with Red Hair all have New Zealand settings;
most of them had been published originally in various journals,
mainly in The Bulletin, and three of them, including the title
piece, had been included in successive volumes of Coast to Coast
—an annual anthology of best Australasian short stories.

The sense of place is strong in his New Zealand stories: there
is of course the flavor given by the leaven of poetic Maori names
—the beaches of Waitara and Ngamotu, the white cliffs of
Pukearuhe—but there is always insistent his love of the countryside of his boyhood which he limns powerfully and evocatively,
as in "The Whare":

It was good to be able to walk freely. The road wound along a
ridge from which the ragged country, broken into gullies and patch-
worked with leaden tea-tree and an occasional acre of ploughed land
or yellowish grass, fell with the slow sweep of a glacier into the
shallow harbour of Kaipara. The water, so far away, had lost its
quick sparkle and become some new element more like metal, a sheet
of silvery tinfoil among the gigantic hills.

(69)

Now there is more to this than Stewart's lifelong empathy
with the outdoors, a sort of pantheism that illumines much of
his poetry and descriptive writing. Rather, since he was born
and raised in a New Zealand rural community at a time when

---

* Page numbers for quotations following refer to these editions respectively.

114

it was still slowly emerging from a state of settlement, still un-sophisticated by contemporary standards, his attitudes in writing about his youthful days represent the drift of a relatively unformed society. It is society at such a stage, or in a state of crisis or fragmentation, which peculiarly has nourished the short story—as we see in Russia, America, and Ireland. And Muriel Bradbrook, writing on the literature of the British Commonwealth in *Literature in Action* (London, 1972), has already noted that the short story is the special form of literature that has met the needs of New Zealand culture. "The maturity of a literature," she writes, "depends on the discovery of a characteristic form—not a theme, not a vocabulary, but an approach. Sharp contrast of certainty in uncertainty that issues in the short story has given a voice to the islands."

Stewart, like his contemporary New Zealand writers, wrote of life and circumstances that had not turned his subjects into the novelist's solid pudding—they existed rather as scattered ingredients. A killer dog on the rampage, a sensitive and moving account of an old man growing old in a little country town, the pleasures of fishing, whether for eels or trout, the day-by-day life of a Maori family—there are a diversity of subjects observed faithfully, but uncluttered by the need to merge them into a novelistic whole.

I Short Stories

It is therefore interesting to note that "A Girl with Red Hair," which is the title story, and the longest of the collection, has been described by the Australian academic and critic, R. G. Howarth, as a "compressed novel"—that because of this, Stewart's technique was most at fault and that the solution would have been to make a novel of it.[1] It is undoubtedly a "long" short story, running to thirty-seven pages, but I do not believe that disqualifies it in any way, and Stewart himself has remarked that in his view, "short" to describe a short story means "just whatever length is right to dramatize a single theme or episode."[2]

The story is about Leila, a girl of singular beauty, growing up in the squalid part of a small town—her father an abatoir worker, illiterate and addicted to drink, content to live near his place of work so that "the smell of boiling flesh, sickly but familiar, blew about the house and loitered in the veranda where he lay, soothing him with a sense of the stability of his universe..." (1). Her discontent grows with her increasing understanding of her social position; she is expected to find companionship in her own class but is merely patronized or sought after as someone who might become available, by the moneyed young men who are regarded as the town's "upper" class. Her sense of shame and her parents' lowly circumstances and the meanness of life in their cottage where it is necessary for her to live, conflict with her vision of the horizons offered as her social life extends. This leads, with the ordinary tensions of adolescence, to outbursts of emotional instability—sensitively and sympathetically conveyed by Stewart in his narrative as he describes her feeling for a working youth of her own class whom she eventually marries:

> In her imagination the stench of the abatoirs filled the bedroom and choked her. She believed that the sickening odour had poisoned all her days; she had breathed it and loathed it as a child and she breathed it and retched at it now. Only Maisie really loved her and told her about her hair.
> Gathering the thick silk of it into her hands, Leila cried in her mind, "And it is beautiful! I will be beautiful! I'll show them all."
> She began to think about Les and saw that she would lose him if she trifled with him much longer. "Who cares?" she muttered.
> At the thought of his frank desire that persisted, domineering, harsh and contemptuous even when she had manoeuvred him into the wheedling he so detested, she was flooded with an emotion so fierce and contradictory that she wanted at once to bite and scratch and stamp and hiss with rage—to lash her hand across the wild sullen image of his face—and to weep for joy at the sweetness of life, the adorable mystery of her being, the beauty of her slight body and burning, heavy hair.
> I don't want to lose him, she thought in anguish. I've got nobody. I could die and nobody would care. I don't want to lose him!

(11)

Once she is married, the dull routine of her domestic life and the monotonous and unfamiliar regimen of raising her baby son affect her relationship with her dull and unimaginative husband. She sees no escape from a situation not dissimilar to the encircling circumstances of her childhood. The dream has gone, the reality is with her seemingly for the rest of her life— Stewart again is pursuing one of his favorite themes. Skilfully he conveys to us Leila's mental struggle to reduce the vague concept of "life" to a consistent and manageable entity that she can comprehend. But then her second child is born—a girl with red hair—and life at last, suddenly and dramatically, has brought its true meaning to her in this promise of her own re-birth, a new cycle of living of which she can be a part:

"She'll be the one for the boys!" the nurse cried, laughing to see Leila so happy.
Leila laughed too. She held the child as high as she could, brandishing the little bundle in her two hands. Her peals of wild laughter in which sobs were mingled, hysterical trumpets of triumph and scorn and liberation, rang against the white-washed walls and frightened the pretty nurse. She moved to take the child away, but the mother would not give it up. "No," she said, "she's mine."

(37)

This "long short story" remains one of the best in Australian literature—because Stewart triumphantly keeps within its bounds in tracing Leila's physical and psychological development; if he has to telescope incidents and time-passages he does this by showing the life of the town and its people keeping pace with Leila's growing up; indeed Stewart's management of time is artistically and acceptably conveyed. It is a story that can be reread with consistent enjoyment. And if it can be argued that "there was ample material for a novel"[3] in this story, then this fact in itself is a simple argument for Stewart's achievement in carrying off his subject *as* a short story. He has, in short, ac-complished the near impossible—he has satisfied exhaustively in writing briefly. After all, the novelist is concerned with many things; the short-story writer, with one thing or theme that implies many. Singularity and intensity are the essence of his art. It is the marked personal attitude in Stewart's writing that demonstrates these qualities, and he gives a further striking illustration of these powers in his story "The Whare."

Here again the theme is simple, uncomplicated, direct. A

young man drifts into a Maori settlement and becomes the guest of an old Maori couple in their primitive hut, or "whare." At first he finds it strange and exhilarating to share their simple lifestyle; then comes a sympathy and a genuine feeling for the people themselves.

I began to understand something of Maori hospitality and of their outlook on life, simple but realistic, tolerant but not sentimental. It arose partly from the fact that understanding was easier than anger.

(74)

But in the end there edges into his consciousness a restlessness, an unease, even a sense of foreboding:

I looked at the old couple, nodding by the fire, the light on their dark faces. What did I really know about them? What went on in those secretive Maori minds? They weren't animals. They had their own thoughts, based on a conception of life beyond my understanding. What possible communion could there be between the white man and the native? The memory of that deep, mindless sympathy when we sat quietly by the fire on the wet night was uncannily disturbing, horrible. The friendly little whare was a prison

(78)

One night he silently leaves the whare, and continues his wanderings.

It is beautifully compact, Chekhovian, in fact, because while there is intense visualization of the scene within the whare and of the settlement itself, the social surroundings do not in any way lessen Stewart's capacity to look closely into the hearts of the Maori couple and of the narrator (the young man) himself. This is in part, I suspect, because Stewart admits that the story is based on a personal experience.[4] But it is especially true in this story as it is in others in this collection, notably "Give Us This Day" (a moving portrait of an old man, going about his daily round) and "He's Going to Use That Scythe" (about an illiterate, taciturn farm laborer whom loneliness and isolation have driven to the edge of madness), that we identify ourselves with Stewart's glance or vision—so much is projected which is not actually put down. In each of these stories so far referred to there is a wholly convincing—so much so that we accept it as truthful—exploration of a complete consciousness of life. As can be seen from the quotations already given, Stewart's prose, in this context, is severe and exact. His ironies are subtle but hard to the point of being pitiless (but only, we realize afterwards, in the interests of realism), as we see in the relationship between the small boy and the old man, Brewster, in "Give Us This Day":

> "How old are you, Mr Brewster?" the boy asked him as they paused at the corner for breath.
> "Eh?" said Mr Brewster absently.
> He was past the age at which he could be troubled to answer the questions of a small boy, should the question happen to penetrate the fog of his mentality. It was only in his faint sense of discomfort, indeed, that he recognized his companion as belonging to the same species. For the most part, he accepted the phenomenon of the boy at his side as he would have accepted a dog at his heels.
> The boy did not repeat the question. After the fiasco of their first journey together, when remark after remark had dropped to the ground like a stunned bird from the blank wall of Mr Brewster's somnolence, he had practically given up the effort of making conversation. He, too, in the depths of his mind, was aware that the mountain of years that towered between them made communication impossible. Mr Brewster was not a man like his father, who, though peculiar, inhabited the same universe. He was something fabulous, like an elephant at the circus.

(100–101)

Stewart illustrates also in some of his short stories his often-expressed view, in his critical writings, of the importance of humor and comedy in creative writing. He wrote once in a review in the *Bulletin's* "Red Page":

Australian short story writers, fortunately, seem to be turning to comedy these days. The great gloom which fell upon English short story writers with the rise of leftism and which perhaps reached its nadir in H. E. Bates' collection *The Beauty of the Dead*—a wail of misery from cover to cover—cast its shadow over Australian and New Zealand writing in recent years. Given just a trifle more imagination Australian short story writers are on the right track. Those who have

been writing comedy for the *The Bulletin* and *Coast to Coast* share
with Eudora Welty a warm love of humanity in its errors as well as
its virtues; a detached, gently ironical outlook; a keen appreciation
of those oddities or quirks of character which bring colour and
diversity to the human scene; and a strong sense for local colour
born of the knowledge, conscious or unconscious, that a genuine
love of humanity is shown not in vague idealism about China or
Peru but in affection for the places and people one knows.[5]

If these can be thought of as postulates, then nowhere are they
better illustrated than in another of Stewart's stories in this
book—"Carnival." It tells of the two "naughty ladies" of a
small town—Mrs. Trotter and Fat Hilda (". . . established in the
town, as much a local institution as the Oddfellows Lodge or
the half-wit who met all the trains and strutted in front of the
town bank on occasions of ceremony") (40), and the reluctant
duty of the local sergeant of police and his assistant officer, to
warn them of complaints made against them. Sergeant Piggott
is delightfully drawn—"years of presiding over the moral welfare
of a small town had given [him] something of the appearance
and all of the patriarchal somnolence of a Black Orpington
rooster among its hens" (40).

Stewart uses the animal show, or fair, as the backdrop to his
story. Mrs. Trotter and Fat Hilda, arrayed in their finery, roam
through the fairgrounds, patronizing the sideshows, admiring
the exhibits; Sergeant Piggott and his assistant, Constable Yates,
catch sight of them now and then—the sergeant uncertain to the
point of unwillingness about exercising his authority. Stewart
catches all the bustle, jollity, and excitement of the scene, and
uses a montage effect to continue the action of the story; just
as Bloom in Joyce's *Ulysses* catches sight, at various points in
his saunterings through the streets of Dublin, of the screwed-up
handbill ("Elijah is Coming") bobbing about in the River
Liffey, so the pair of women, appearing every now and then
to the view of the two policemen, give the necessary continuity
to a story delightful in its humor and humanity:

"Roll up, bowl up, tumble up!" a stocky attendant was shouting
by the merry-go-round. "Any more for the next ride? The last ride
of the day. Who's gonna ride on the merry-go-round?"

" 'Ere," said Fat Hilda. "Gimme a ticket."

"There's the sergeant," whispered Mrs Trotter warningly.

"The old cow!" said Fat Hilda. "I bleeve 'e's follering' us!"

On his way to the gates to watch the homeward tide of traffic, Sergeant Piggott stood spellbound.

Fat Hilda, mounted on a red wooden horse with staring eyes, rode it like a Valkyrie. Its decoration ravaged by the heat and industry of the day, her face was bare and flushed; her beady eyes shone with delight; her dress billowed as she flew. Surprising himself, Sergeant Piggott chuckled. The face flashed into view, then out of sight again, and into view and out of sight like a crazy acceleration of day and night. Fat Hilda shrieked, clasped her arms about the neck of her steed, and spun triumphantly among the music.

"She's a beaut, ain't she?" said Mick Yates. "What you goin' to do about 'em?"

"We'll see," said the sergeant.

(50–51)

In the end, it is only when evening comes that the policemen decide to visit the home of the ladies to convey the "complaint." In so doing, they startle into flight the "customer" of the moment —none other than Mr. Royland, the president of the Agricultural and Pastoral Association, the most important man of that important day. The policemen are invited in:

A sense of homeliness and comfort stole over the sergeant as he gazed about him. The stove, black and polished, sent out a companionable glow. Cards and an unopened bottle of beer stood on the table and half a dozen more bottles paraded in a row along the sink.

"We been 'avin' a little game of cards," said Fat Hilda.

"You bet!" said Mick Yates.

The sergeant grunted. All the long roads that day had led to this room. While the stove shone and glowed and the light struck golden on the bottles and Fat Hilda smirked and Mrs Trotter gazed at him in calm inquiry—for she could not believe that the visit portended anyything worse than a warning—the sergeant found it hard to say what had to be said.

(55)

And so the sergeant and his henchman are tempted, and fall.

"Come on, Yatesey," said Mrs Trotter, gazing merrily into the dark, dancing eyes of the constable. "Take your helmet off and make yourself comfortable."

The constable winked.

"Umm," said Sergeant Piggott slowly. "I don't suppose a little game, just to pass the time away, would do us any harm."

"Oh, you dirty old man!" cried Fat Hilda delightedly.

Gently she lifted the sergeant's helmet from his large, bald head and placed it upside-down among the shining bottles on the sink.

(57)

Here again, though the theme is predominantly humorous in concept and intention, Stewart's mastery of the medium is always apparent—the gift of seeing people and events in the changing moments of the day, so that every detail is spontaneous, unchanged observation. The effect is that he seems not to be telling a story by letting his readers see through the superficial story into what is happening inside the people as it goes on: the indecision of the policemen, the holiday mood and abandon of the two women. And the end is left open, as it were, so that we *know* that the lives of these people in the small town, after the incidents of the day, will go on exactly the same as before.

Only one story in the collection is out of tune, as it were— "The Medium"—where a couple of tricksters are exposed, and where one has the impression that Stewart is writing out of invention rather than observation, and, at that, unconvincingly. But for the rest his stories are thoroughly planted. There is throughout them a warm feeling for his New Zealand countryside and its towns; a generous understanding and compassion for the people who live there; a poet's ear for their speech and conversations; and a poet's evocation of their experiences and emotions.

II *Miscellaneous Short Stories*

Of the several stories he wrote in Australia after publication of *A Girl with Red Hair,* each with an Australian background, the best is certainly "The Three Jolly Foxes," later included in *Coast to Coast* (Sydney, 1946).* More than any other of his

---

* Page numbers for quotations following refer to this edition.

stories it indicates what heights Stewart might have scaled had he kept to this genre. Here, in a study of human psychology, brittle with menace, steeped in unpleasantness, Stewart deserts his philosophy about humor, unless we could use the term "black" humor. The first of the foxes is a real fox heading for the rabbit—traps set by Joe Packet, who runs a small farm and a roadhouse at Fat Chow Creek on the road to Melbourne.

Joe is like a fox, too; he lies snug with his vixen in the warm burrow of the bed, but all night long he leaves his mouth out in the paddock to catch the rabbits; his spare mouth, his dozen spare mouths, all gaping, waiting, with sharp steel teeth. Joe Packet has caught two rabbits while he sleeps. Broken, they lie in his spare steel mouths —fast shut these mouths are. How warm, how appetizing they smell! How inviting is the thought of pink flesh under that soft grey fur— The red fox lolls his tongue. He whines with pleasure.

(176)

But the red fox is caught in a trap, and Joe in the morning kills and skins it as the third fox arrives—a businessman, Mr. Hardcastle ("You can tell he's a fox by the bark of his laughter. ...Bark! Bark! Bark!"), with a rabbit in his mouth, "the new Mrs. Hardcastle—brand new: only last night—snuggling beside him in her cony-seal coat." The wily small fox Joe Packet outwits the big barking fox Mr. Hardcastle, by charging him double for his breakfast, and selling him a parcel of groceries at an inflated price. Stewart carries this remarkable mélange of human and animal, the imagery brilliantly interlocking, right to the spine-chilling end, when Mr. Hardcastle sets off again on his journey with his forty-year-old rabbit—his ex-secretary ("Why marry her then? And after ten years. Well, we grow old. Time, loneliness and—the dark thing. A widower in a dark house..."). Mr. Hardcastle admits that the cunning fox Packet and his vixen have tricked him, but laughs his hearty bark-laugh in admiration, as from one fox to another.

"You're a bit of a fox yourself," says Mrs. Hardcastle softly. She looks at him archly, over the rims of her glasses. "But you want to look out, you know. More than one old fox has put his foot right into a rabbit-trap. And that was the end of him." Her wedding-bells peal and peal.

Mr. Hardcastle begins to laugh, then does not. He stares at his brand-new wife. There is something strangely steel-like in Mrs. Hardcastle's appearance. Bones, wires, those horn-rimmed glasses, that frizz of springs on her head, those enormous teeth. And the old fox in a trap. He stamps his foot on the accelerator.

(183)

I have read nothing quite like this story in Australian literature: certainly it is in this very story more than in any other he has written that he comes closest to his own prescription that

normally we expect a short story to be an illumination of some human experience, rather than a mere 'tale' or 'yarn' where facts are all-important. One looks for the compact form and the clear spark of life in it: and of course, the finer the mind from which it emanates, the finer the sparkle we shall get.[6]

Stewart here reached the level of writing that makes the short story a memorable art, so that it stays whole in the mind; a way of writing as excellent as the sonnet, the ballad or the play; as piercing as a piece of music or sculpture; as evocative as a watercolor. On the one hand, it is a great pity that Stewart stopped writing short stories at this point: on the other, he was early in his thirties at this time, and since the short-story writer is a strange mixture of poet, reporter, and aphorist (all this is true of Stewart) and a short-breathed writer to boot, his best work will undoubtedly be done while he is young, and so it was in this case.

III   The Seven Rivers

There are several fishing stories in A Girl with Red Hair—including "Stan," "The Eel Fisher," and "The Hare's Ear"—each of which reflects a more than ordinary knowledge of the pastime. In fact Stewart is a dedicated fisherman and has been all his life, fishing the streams of his native New Zealand and his adopted Australia. Most of his holidays and leisure hours have seen him engaged in this occupation, and he has made these varied experiences the basis of The Seven Rivers (Sydney, 1966).

It is an unusual book, a collection of essays gracefully and stylishly written, and it is one of those rare books which reflects truly and faithfully the personality of its author. For Stewart is an unassuming and modest man, but with a keen mind, who will quietly and persuasively present his point of view and who delights to convey to others in conversation or opinion the things and experiences that delight him. *The Seven Rivers* is correspondingly an unassuming but wholly delightful and unusual book, full of humor and observations about life and people. In its varying aspects it is contemplative, reminiscent, descriptive and autobiographical.

Basically it is about fishing. It takes its title from seven coastal rivers which were in the vicinity of Eltham in New Zealand where Stewart spent his boyhood. Their names, he writes, "were a tangle of Maori polysyllables, wild as the ferns and blackberries that clung to their yellow clay banks, sweet as the water that bubbled over their stones: the Waingongoro, the Mangatoki, the Kapuni, the Kaupokonui, the Tangatara, Mangahume, and Waiau" (11). They were all trout streams, and Stewart was no exception to the probability that anyone who lived near them became, by attraction, a fisherman. But the book takes in not only his fishing (and hunting) experiences in New Zealand—the last few essays tell of his adventures with his friends in Australian rivers scarcely less euphoniously named— the Duckmaloi, the Badja, the Goodrabidgee, the Murrumbidgee, and the Snowy River.

Fishing is to Stewart at once an art and a philosophy. As for its art, fishing means trout fishing—"the solitary trout, whose capture . . . is the drama of one man against one fish, seen rising or feeding in his clear element and fished for with all the skill and finesse at your command" (4). And in fishing as in any other art, Stewart maintains that "mankind demands a conclusion to its dramas so that, at least within the limited area selected for the battleground, the universe may make sense" (3). He carries this idea forward into one of his best poems, "The Fisherman," where he merges it with his view of civilization at large and in time:

> fisherman stand
> For the men who stood like rock in the dark of history
> For the men who will stand like rock in the dark of the future. . . .
>   (275)

Nevertheless, within these larger concepts, Stewart's sense of humor keeps the pursuit of fishing within proper perspectives: "It is surely pleasant occasionally, when fishing, to catch fish..."; and he is well aware of the idiosyncrasies and eccentricities of fishermen (which make up many charming anecdotes in this book)—all of whom hold, for instance, the belief "that the fishing is always better Further On. In fact Further On is the only possible place to fish" (194).

Stewart has allowed a good deal of autobiographical detail to stray into the book, some of it of incidental intelligence, some of it much more valuable to our understanding of him. He recalls boyhood idylls in the picturesque country around his home town of Eltham—fishing and catching eels in its streams, feasting on trout and ducks cooked over campfires, picnicking on splendid beaches, playing truant from school, and building a secret hut where

at ease we boiled in a kerosene tin the eels we caught from the stream, invariably very thin and black with silver bellies, tasting deliciously: at ease roved the bush and the neighbouring farmlands, stealing green lemons or eating *kinkis* which are the fleshy centre of some parasitical growth on native trees, reputed to have been enjoyed by the Maoris...

(45)

He tells of his days at New Plymouth High School: there are memorable portraits of schoolteachers, and, in retrospect, the stirring of a writer's observation and the storing of experiences:

Our metropolis had a population of about two thousand; but even there the most surprising things used to happen. A farmer put gelignite into the oven to blow up his relatives; a respectable citizen in the Government service crept round by night and stole ladies' underwear from their clothes-lines; an Assyrian in Bath Street, heated by love, belaboured his rival with a dog-chain; a strange man put a notice on his house, "Beware of the Lion's Cub." There were fires, even murders; and, just downstream from Bridger Park, the wildest of wild Irishmen started to dig a tunnel which led under the Bank of New South Wales, where he proposed to blow up the strongroom— a large and mighty venture, so it loomed in our childhood, opening

the door to a world of power and desperation beyond anything we
had dreamed of.

(32)

Not surprisingly, then, we see the young Stewart subsequently
as cub reporter on the local newspaper, the Eltham *Argus*, and
later the Stratford *Evening Post*.

This gift for observation was building the storehouse for his
nature poetry—a storehouse which he continued to fill in his
middle years. One of the delights of *The Seven Rivers* is Stewart's wholehearted involvement in the sights and sounds of the
countryside as he describes them. He sees nature red in tooth
and claw in graphic descriptions of a wild cat, spitting and
scratching as it defends its young against a swooping eagle; and
in the scene of a stoat attacking a rabbit. He is moved by the
plight of fleeing animals before an Australian bushfire—wombats,
rabbits, wallabies, snakes, even "hundreds of exhausted bees
crawling about on the wet sand... waiting for the cool of
evening to revive them" (134). He delights in the frolicking of
magpies sliding down the wet leaves of gumtrees after a storm—
"like skiers on a snow-slope or boys on a muddy hillside" (146).
There are rare glimpses of platypuses and yellow-bellied water
rats and "a spiny ant-eater, the echidna, stumbling and rasping
its way along a landslide of broken granite" (213).

Apart from its wholly enchanting artlessness as a personal
chronicle, the joy of this book is equally in the greater understanding of Stewart the poet that emerges from its reading.
He is everlastingly fascinated by the colors of nature whether
it is of the flying possums, the phalangers seen at night: "their
fur silver when we turned the torch on them; their eyes, a soft
opaline blue if you see them by day glowed red like rubies"
(156), or of the landscape in the Snowy River country, "blue
and silver to the sky, shivering in the slightest breeze, rimmed
with low banks where alpine daisies glittered like snowflakes
among the flowering heath, and guineaflowers and bulbine lilies,
with minute white orchids among them, shone gold and yellow
like the sun" (198). Much of this he has transmuted into
his poetry.

The Seven Rivers serves to confirm, then, that Stewart's pre-
eminence among contemporary nature poets arises not from the

imitation of predecessors or from any poetic posing, but from the most genuine love imaginable for what he has seen in mountains, in streams, in forests, and on plains. For who else but a poet could have written the magnificently evocative passages with which he concludes his book, where he describes his efforts, high up on the ramparts of Mt. Kosciusko in the rugged ranges of southeastern New South Wales, to discover the source of the Snowy River:

It was not one stream, but a hundred. It was a patch of bog and buttercups. It was a hole in the heath, filled with clear water, beside which lay the claws of a long-dead yabbie [crayfish], still purple and green despite the weathering by sun and snow. It was a wide watery shallow, unconnected so far as you could see with any direct movement of the stream, lying aimlessly among speckled boulders and the dark-green carpet of heath as if the country could not make up its mind whether to be land or water.

All you could do in this maze of water and flowers—the shiny yellow buttercups, the giant dandelions, the purple eyebright, the silver snow-daisies, the billy-buttons, the creamy sprays and green fronds of the alpine parsley, the exquisite mauve-flowered dwarf mintbush—was to pick one trickle and follow it. On went the trickle through the heath, straight to the final wall; and there, in the little sunlit pool where the snow thrust over the boulders and turned into water before your eyes, surely lay the source of the Snowy. But no; five yards or so beyond it, lay another little pool; and another again beyond it. There was no saying which was the source. Far up the mountainside soaks of melted snow lay hidden among the moss; water gleamed on the granite. The whole mountain was the source. But in and out of the sunlight and the shadowy caverns of the snow in those final crystalline pools, climbing up the mountain as far as a fish could well climb, darted tiny rainbow trout. What a long way they had to go before they grew into four-pounders at the mouth of Wollondilly Creek!

(218)

CHAPTER 5

Douglas Stewart as Editor/Critic

I As Editor: Influence of A. G. Stephens on the Bulletin's Literary Policies

DOUGLAS Stewart's chief work as an editor was when he was in charge of the literary pages of the Australian *Bulletin* between 1940 and 1960—the famous "Red Page," once described as "a literary feature which has had a lasting influence on Australian literature."[1]

The *Bulletin* had been founded in 1880 by J. F. Archibald and John Hayes from a small printing office in Castlereagh Street, Sydney, with a capital of £140, some cases of battered type, and an option on an old and rusty printing machine. Archibald was the driving force in building it up as a national journal. The son of a country policeman with journalistic experience in bush newspapers, he was twenty-four years old when he started the *Bulletin*. From the beginning he dictated its editorial policy, which was a mixture of chauvinism and radical reform: it advocated republicanism, the total secularization of education, and the abandonment of English titles, and denounced imperialism and religious interference with politics. It soon became known as the "bushman's bible" and circulated throughout the settled areas of Australia.

But above all, the journal soon became the repository for what was original in Australian writing of the time. Archibald in taking over the literary with the general editorship, as it were, "without any fixed standards in literature ... had a sure instinct for work that showed literary vision,"[2] and soon he had made his journal the center of Australian creative writing of the day. It was Archibald who, convinced of the genius of a young coach-painter, Henry Lawson, encouraged him to become a regular contributor; Archibald who published A. B. "Banjo" Paterson's first ballad, "The Bush Fire," in 1886; and as well the famous convict stories of William Astley ("Prince Warung"), and stories and poems by Victor Daley, Edward Dyson, and others who were to form the vanguard of Australia's most remarkable literary period, "the 1890s."

In 1894 Archibald, with his infallible nose for a good man, attracted to the *Bulletin's* staff. A. G. Stephens, another country journalist who at the age of twenty-nine had established himself as a fearless and polemical political writer. Soon after he joined the staff Stephens suggested that the familiar red covers of the *Bulletin* should comprise its literary section; but he was not able to put his ideas into effect and institute the "Red Page"[3] until 1896, when he was appointed the *Bulletin's* first literary editor—a position he held for ten years. Apart from the frequent contributions he made himself under his initials "A.G.S." he built on the foundations established by Archibald, developing a further school of Australian writers including Arthur Hoey Davis ("Steele Rudd"), Randolph Bedford, Louis Becke, E. J. Brady, Barbara Baynton, Barcroft Boake, and others. Stephens's single-minded aim was to encourage a distinctively Australian expression in literature, which accorded with Archibald's original objectives. But Stephens had traveled extensively in America and Europe; he had read widely in the classical and contemporary literatures of those countries; accordingly he brought to his editorship a critical armory which not only distinguished his assessment of contemporary writing but enabled him the more effectively to give advice and assistance to the *Bulletin's* by now famous stable of young writers. In addition to his editorial work for the journal he selected, edited, and saw through the press over twenty volumes in the so-called "Books of the Bulletin"—publications launched by the journal. These included such memorable contributions to Australian literature as *Such Is Life* by "Tom Collins" (Joseph Furphy) and *On Our Selection* by "Steele Rudd." After leaving the *Bulletin* in 1906 Stephens continued as a writer, publisher, and lecturer for nearly thirty years—but he will always be revered as the first and perhaps the greatest of "Red Page" editors.

II *Douglas Stewart's Editorship of the* The Bulletin's "Red Page"

Stewart had been contributing occasional verse and short stories to the *Bulletin* from New Zealand for nearly ten years when he was invited by the then literary editor, Cecil Mann (one of Australia's best-known short-story writers), to take a job as the *Bulletin*'s staff light verse writer in 1933 in succession to André Heywood. Stewart came to Australia, but Heywood decided not to retire from his position, and after six months of free-lance work, Stewart returned to New Zealand. In 1937 Stewart went to England, and when he was again offered a job as a staff writer on the *Bulletin* by Mann, he returned to Australia in 1938—and found himself acting as an assistant to Mann. He succeeded to the literary editorship in 1940.

Stewart recalls[4] that even during these wartime years, there were exciting developments in Australian literature, and though the journals *Meanjin* and *Southerly* were just beginning, the *Bulletin* was still the center of the cultural life of the country. This was not to say that some of those concerned with the journal's management were not opposed to the literary side of the magazine, which they felt reduced the journal's "selling" capacity. But on the whole Stewart was given editorial freedom to review and print what he thought best in literature, and to write as he chose. So it was, he remembers

... because the writers too recognized it as the centre, the only place they could get published, we met everybody who was worth knowing and tremendous people used to just walk in the door. I remember seeing Miles Franklin and Mary Gilmore one day appear like a couple of giantesses or goddesses or something in the doorway; Daisy Bates darting down the corridor sometimes popped in to see us. And then Judith Wright coming in as a young writer, and Rosemary Dobson quivering like a leaf with nervousness with her first poem, Francis Webb arriving and bringing those exciting things "Ben Boyd" and "Leichhardt", John Tierney ("Brian James"), who was not my discovery but I soon acquired him, coming in and bringing his stories.[5]

To read through the "Red Pages" for the twenty years of Stewart's editorship is to comprehend a personal achievement on

his part that is very difficult, because of its magnitude, to sum-
marize adequately. One realizes over these years how impossible it would have been to have kept track of currents, not only
in Australian but in English, American and some Continental
literatures, without reading the pages of the *Bulletin.* The poetry
of Auden, Day Lewis, T. S. Eliot, the Sitwells, Stephen Spender,
Robert Frost; the novels of Thomas Mann, Aldous Huxley,
James Joyce, J. C. Powys; important literary texts such as Eliot's
edition of Kipling's poetry, new editions of Boswell's *Journals*;
important anthologies of prose and verse—very little escaped
Stewart's net. Children's literature, Australian as well as overseas, was always featured; there were regular notes on Aus-
tralian art, theater, music, and ballet. But certainly no work of
any consequence in Australian or New Zealand literature, that
I can see, was overlooked. And this was a period when many
notable Australian books appeared. There was the poetry of
Kenneth Slessor, R. D. FitzGerald, Judith Wright, Francis Webb,
Mary Gilmore, A. D. Hope; novels by Patrick White, T. A. G.
Hungerford, and Christina Stead; short-story collections by
Brian James, David Campbell, E. O. Schlunke, and Frank Dalby
Davison.

In the reviews of these books Stewart's editorial insistence on
certain approaches can be clearly seen. He has always held that
the job of the reviewer is to "display" the book: "you say what
it's about and you give a brief opinion whether you liked it or
not, and you don't skither about on stage in front of the reader
either."[6] Where Stewart permitted longer critical pieces (there
was usually one long essay in each "Red Page") it was clear
that he invited contributors to deal with writers they liked,
rather than to write destructively on writers they did not like,
a philosophy he personally followed in his own longer articles.

No critical work of any significance on Australian literature
escaped Stewart's editorial attention. It so happened during
these years that a number of studies appeared which reflected
especially an academic awareness of the growing importance of
indigenous writing, and Stewart, in his columns, was quick to
seize on these and emphasize their appearance as critical mile-
stones. A. A. Phillips's *The Australian Tradition* (1943) gave
Stewart the opportunity to editorialize about the tendency in

Australian literature "to value reformist politics at the expense of creative achievement."[7] Vincent Buckley's *Essays in Poetry* (1957) was the occasion for Stewart to applaud as "flawless" Buckley's definition of poetry as that it "dealt with man at a metaphysical level."[8] The appearance of Brian Elliott's critical study and biography of Marcus Clarke led to the "Red Page" comment[9] of the too-common faults of so much Australian biographical writing—tendencies to diffuseness and sentimentality, and to overmuch concern with the writer's period rather than with a clear focus on the man himself. The treatment the "Red Page" gave to such famous Australian novels as Clarke's *For the Term of His Natural Life*, Tom Collins's *Such Is Life*, Henry Kingsley's *Geoffrey Hamlyn* when, from time to time, these appeared in reprint, repeatedly underlined Stewart's editorial conviction that the word "classic" to describe books such as these needed the strictest qualification. "Unless the term classic means a novel that could take its place, on its own intrinsic merits, among the great books of the world's literature, it has no right to that august description." The "Red Page" frequently deplored the tendency of literary historians to apply the term with "a genial inexactitude"[10] to describe any well-known novel, consistently reprinted, which was of interest to the Australian reader as a period piece.

III *Editorial Innovations and Encouragement of Australian Writers*

One of Stewart's editorial innovations in the "Red Page" (now regularly the custom in present-day journals) was to assign his principal reviews to writers whom he felt had special authority and knowledge to deal with a particular work. Thus M. H. Ellis became a regular contributor of critical studies and reviews of Australian historical works; W. E. FitzHenry and Colin Roderick dealt with earlier writers; Nancy Keesing with ballads and balladists; W. W. Stone with books of bibliographical interest, and so on. Stewart frequently called on Norman Lindsay to contribute forthright essays on all aspects of Australian art and literature, and others, who had similar "roving commissions," so to speak, included Ronald McCuaig, Hugh

Anderson, Cecil Mann, and David Campbell. The result was that the "Red Page" gained a prestige and authority in the field of literature and art which has not since been equalled in equivalent pages of any Australian journal of a general type (i.e., as distinct from a completely literary journal such as *Meanjin Quarterly* or *Southerly*).

Stewart supplemented his determination to raise the critical standards of his country's literature by the encouragement of young poets and short-story writers, as well as by the consistent publication of those who were well established in their field. So it was that in the *Bulletin* over these years one can find, in poetry, the emerging work of Rosemary Dobson, Judith Wright, and James McAuley, side by side with regular writing by R. D. FitzGerald, Hugh McCrae, Mary Gilmore, and the New Zealanders Arnold Wall and William Hart-Smith. The proof of the pudding is in the eating, and Stewart's achievement in fostering the writing of Australian poetry during the years of his "Red Page" editorship can be seen in the acknowledgments listed in the many poetry anthologies published in more recent years. His "discoveries" make a formidable list—in addition to poets such as Rosemary Dobson (mentioned above), they included Francis Webb, John Blight, David Campbell, and Eric Rolls. Among short-story writers of these years whom Stewart encouraged not only by publishing their work but by offering frank, critical advice, may be listed Brian James, E. O. Schlunke, Thelma Forshaw, and Margaret Trist: their work appeared side by side with stories by established writers such as Norman Lindsay, Cecil Mann, Les Robinson, Vance Palmer, Frank Dalby Davison, and many others. Nothing like this efflorescence of Australian writing has occurred since in any general journal or magazine.

IV *Achievement as "Red Page" Editor*

It is probably no coincidence that when Stewart relinquished the literary editorship of the *Bulletin* in 1960 the journal lost much of its literary character and significance, becoming in the years that followed more of "a magazine that somehow concerns itself day-to-day with Vietnam, Foreign Investment, White

Australia, the Brain Drain and everything from the suicide rate to race relations in New Guinea," as a later editor[11] described it.

If Stewart was the last of the important line of literary editors of the *Bulletin*, historically he has laid claim to be bracketed with A. G. Stephens as the most influential and talented of them. Writing of A. G. Stephens in *The Legend of the Nineties*, Vance Palmer had remarked:

His chief value to the *Bulletin*, however, proved to be his faculty for discovering, among the host of contributors, those men who had something to say and bringing them forward. His literary judgment was sound, and its edge had been sharpened by contact with the best contemporary writing of England and France; he could distinguish what was interesting but ephemeral from what had more permanent worth. By nature he was robust, with an interest in men as well as in books, and a love for whatever was salty, indigenous, and charged with the country's character. He was not to be deceived by superficial slickness and was able to detect the original quality in work that was outwardly crude, like Steele Rudd's first sketches of life on a selection. This made him a distinct creative force when the Red Page was reserved for him and he was left free to devote his whole attention to the literature that was emerging.[12]

Nothing in this encomium could not be said of Stewart in the same role: indeed Stewart as a creative writer much more gifted and prolific than Stephens, was able, I believe, to command a greater respect among a generation of writers much more sophisticated and advanced in technique than those with whom Stephens was concerned.

V *Stewart's Work as a Publishing Editor*

Stewart since leaving the *Bulletin* has continued his activities as a literary editor for the oldest and most respected of Australian publishing houses, Angus and Robertson. Here he has been able to put to practical and profitable use the experience gained during his years with the *Bulletin*. He has edited a string of prose and verse anthologies, most of them now accepted as standard works in their field: most notable of these in terms of enduring value to Australian scholars and scholarship are undoubtedly *Australian Bush Ballads* (1955) and *Old Bush Songs*

(1957), which he edited jointly with Nancy Keesing. Very early in his *Bulletin* days he had suggested the idea of annual anthologies of Australian short stories and poetry. This was the genesis of the highly successful *Coast to Coast* series of short-story anthologies which along with Beatrice Davis, Stewart supervised, and the *Australian Poetry* anthologies of which he also assumed the general editorship.

Stewart has always been interested in the ballad form. As I have noted in previous pages he has experimented in the form in his poetry (the *Glencoe* sequence) and in his verse play *Fisher's Ghost*. He had long considered that though the ballad was admittedly more shallow in theme and more elementary in technique than accepted poetry it was not necessarily inferior, and that as in the Border ballads, was often, in fact, exciting and accomplished poetry by any standards. He had become through his early reading of the *Bulletin* (even in his New Zealand days) and of the A. B. Paterson collection *The Old Bush Songs* (1905) and other sources, very much an enthusiast for the Australian bush ballad; as he recalls: "I was always fascinated by them: I thought them unique in the world's literature."[13] He felt that modern collections needed to be made of them, and having enlisted the help of a fellow poet, Nancy Keesing, researched for three years not only among which of these had been published down the years, but by seeking oral transcripts from old bushmen and others who could recite from memory ballads and songs of which there were no written variants extant. Eventually these were published in two volumes mentioned above. *Australian Bush Ballads* comprised a selection from ballads written or orally preserved since the 1860s. Stimulated (as Stewart notes) by Adam Lindsay Gordon—famous horserider and verse writer, whose bust stands in Westminster Abbey's Poets' Corner—the cult of the Australian ballad reached its peak in the 1890s with such writers as Henry Lawson, A. B. ("Banjo") Paterson, and Barcroft Boake. *Old Bush Songs* was subtitled "Rhymes of Colonial Times—enlarged and revised from A. B. Paterson's collection." In it all the early colonial material collected by Paterson was preserved along with the songs and ballads of this period subsequently discovered by Stewart and Nancy Keesing.

Stewart contributed a splendid Preface to the former volume in which he set forth quite clearly the editorial principles he and his coeditor had observed in assembling the collection—the exclusion of anything but the ballad form, the discarding of all forms of street songs and sea chanties (since these were not "bush" ballads), and so on. He also entertainingly and informatively canvassed the theories of the origins of the Australian ballad, demonstrating at the same time his wide reading in the genre with appropriate references to the influence of Bret Harte and Kipling. With dry humor he referred to the suggestion of one Australian authority that the ballad had arisen from the habit of cattle drovers (i.e., herdsmen) "singing to the cattle," to keep the animals from becoming restless. "Of course," observed Stewart, "as the propounder of the theory would recognize, it would not explain the goldfields ballads, unless the fossickers sang to the goats." He advanced his own theory "that the Australian balladists were simply a reincarnation of the old Border rhymers, or at least that the old Scottish power of song, dormant in the blood through the centuries when the clans were subdued and dispersed, leapt to life again in the wild freedom of the new country." Certainly, as he was able to show, Adam Lindsay Gordon, A. B. Paterson, and Will Ogilvie—three of the leaders in the ballad movement—were all of Scottish descent, while the Celtic strain of "old harpers singing again" come to light too in other celebrated balladists of the 1890s of Irish ancestry, such as Roderick Quinn, E. J. Brady, and John O'Brien. "The sum of all these pleasant theories is, I think," Stewart summed up, "simply that the ballad arose in Australia spontaneously. The soil was prepared for it, the men were here to compose it: it sprang from the earth and it flowered."[14] To edit these collections was altogether a labor of love to Stewart, who has never ceased to believe that the bush ballads, taken as a whole, are the most distinctively national statement Australian poetry has yet made.

Stewart has always maintained that the poet Hugh McCrae's (1876–1958) "day must come," as the writer of beautiful lyrics comparable, at his best, to those of such an English poet as George Herrick. Because of this belief he undertook the selecting and editing of McCrae's poems (*Hugh McCrae: Selected*

Poems, 1966). It offers one of the most interesting examples of Stewart's approach as an editor. In an introduction to the collection he notes to his own satisfaction (and by inference, that of his readers) that McCrae's poems carry object lessons which Stewart himself has consistently stressed in his own poems and in his critical writing. First of all, there is the point that no generation of poets can speak the same language as those immediately preceding or succeeding it; there will always be a difference of idiom in language and subject matter. So it is with McCrae (whose generation ended as Stewart's approached) —and so, Stewart is reminding us, it will be with the poets who follow him. Second, Stewart remarks in McCrae's poetry the virtues of "clear, direct speech, the best of poetry," which is a factor which does *not* change, whether from Chaucer to Shakespeare, Shelley to Yeats, or McCrae to Stewart. And third, McCrae demonstrates, as Stewart has tried always to teach, that life—and poetry—should be enjoyable.

Stewart's editorial method in compiling this collection is, because he believes readers of his generation have difficulty in coming to terms with McCrae's poetry, to arrange the poems to relate to certain "paths" which he recommends *his* readers should follow. One path leads to an investigation of the "Australian content" (i.e., subject matter) of the poems; another to the music of the poems ("All through his poetry you will hear the sound of horns or trumpets or bugles or the kindred baying of hounds"). Other paths lead to an appreciation of McCrae's small pieces, or fragments (wherein, Stewart considers, much of McCrae's lyrical magic lies); of examples of his visionary writing and fantasy; and finally of his love poetry. In all this, it is safe to say, Stewart is responsible for one of the most satisfying editions of an Australian poet's verse in recent years, manifestly succeeding in his aim "to represent McCrae at his best . . . to represent him in all his styles and moods."

VI *Editor of Important Anthologies*

It is interesting to note how Stewart has gone about the task of editing a number of anthologies. He wrote once with a good deal of feeling:

The making of a national anthology is, of course, an extraordinarily difficult task. The hardest thing of all, especially for a practising writer, is to look back into the period immediately preceding our own, whose moods and styles and aims were entirely different and to try to decide what living merit remains under the strange costume. . . . Personally, I am inclined to think it is an outrageous and impossible task. You are to a certain extent obliged since you cannot restrict yourself to the half dozen or so assured immortals, and since you have only 150 years of poetry to work on instead of England's long centuries, to deal in false values, presenting works which you know to be patchy or inferior.[15]

Stewart, in so writing, was probably taking a pessimistic view of the task confronting the Australian anthologist. In fact, he has been conspicuously successful in his own ventures, producing at least two anthologies which might be described as definitive texts—*Modern Australian Verse* (1964—reprinted in 1968) and *Short Stories of Australia—The Lawson Tradition* (1967). In his introduction to the former he states in simple and unequivocal terms that in choosing poems for an anthology "one should not lose sight of the true and original meaning of 'enjoyment.' It means giving joy: and in the long run I feel often enough that is what poetry is about." Without deserting the principles that mark the best poetry, like melody and feeling in the lyric and structure and movement in the narrative, he picks out poems that "are alive, odd, humorous, out of the way," confessing thereby in deed as in word his abhorrence of dullness. He has refused to choose poems just because they are about Australia, or poems that "reflect the age"; his anthology sets out to give "as wide a picture as possible, consistent with the policy of Australian poetry of the period." He has declined to confine his poets in categories; he has never felt this can be done any more than to imprison them in a given period of time. He has reiterated the view throughout his critical writing that "all talk about movement means generalization, and all generalizations are inaccurate." The result of all this is the production of one of the most readable and consistently enjoyable collections of poetry yet published in Australia.

His collection of Australian short stories also illustrates his editorial principles. For instance, he refuses necessarily to re-

strict each writer's representation to one story, explaining in his
introduction that this tends to be "levelling and middling"—it
is often much better to allow a writer's range and variety to be
shown by the inclusion of at least two and sometimes three
stories, and this he has done. A story, he stresses, should be
"intrinsically worth telling." His task in preparing the anthology
was, of course, made easier by the mandate to base his selection
on Henry Lawson and writers who have preserved the style
and flavor of Lawson. This meant the eschewing of love stories
and city themes; the preference for stories dealing with man's
battle against and conquest of the inhospitable bush; the
emphasis on dry and often ironical comedy. He has again succeeded admirably; his collection is as valuable to the student
and researcher as it is enjoyable to the ordinary reader. Altogether Stewart richly deserves the tribute paid him by a fellow
writer as "one of the most generously influential of literary
editors."[16]

I As Critic: Critical Principles

Stewart's dedicated work as an editor ran parallel in most
cases with his writing as a literary critic. Indeed, in his editorship
of the "Red Page" the two activities were largely interwoven,
as has already been outlined, and, like A. G. Stephens before
him, Stewart's everyday dealing with writers and his editorial
decision-making combined, in a sense, to hone his critical fac-
ulties. Most of his extant critical writing, therefore, is contained
in the "Red Pages" of the *Bulletin,* some of the earlier part of
which was collected in *The Flesh and the Spirit* (Sydney, 1943).
As well, the prefaces and introductions to anthologies which he
has edited are also useful in assessing his literary opinions, and
he has contributed occasional articles to Australian literary
journals in recent years.

Stewart's principles of criticism are not difficult to ascertain.
He praised the methods of A. G. Stephens, one of his predecessors as editor of the "Red Page"; he remarked once that when
it came to books Stephens knew what he was talking about—
"that simple fact, making him a critic instead of merely a reviewer, is what made his criticism respected in his time and

keeps it alive today."[18] The other principle followed rigorously by Stephens was his refusal to tolerate two standards of criticism —one for European and the other for Australian literature; to relate Australian books to the stream of world literature, however they might suffer by comparison, in Stephens's opinion honored the author as well as doing him justice—and Stewart applauds this and follows it out in his own criticism. As he has himself written: "Comparisons are supposed to be vulgar but they are the basis of all criticism. If a poem by a contemporary Australian writer will not stand up to comparison with the traditional masterpieces of the language, then it is not worth serious discussion."[19] (He made this point when he was comparing the famous elegy "Five Bells" by the Australian poet Kenneth Slessor, with Matthew Arnold's "Thyrsis.")

Stewart prefers to look at a piece of creative writing as a whole: he condemns the "piece-meal" method—"taking a poem to pieces rhyme by rhyme, word by word, syllable by syllable in order to find out exactly what makes it tick... after a while the mind simply refuses to follow...."[20] No better illustration of his generous attitude to the business of criticism can be found than in his strictures on the method that should be followed by the critic of an anthology:

The proper course for the critic is to say whether or not the work satisfactorily fulfils its purpose. Has the editor done his job fairly and within his chosen limits, and with sound judgement? Who's in: who's out? He is not asked to judge the poetry of a nation: he is asked to judge an anthology. Anthologies are at best shopwindows, and the critic needs to be very sure he knows all that is hidden in the shop before he attempts to draw personal conclusions from them.[21]

II *Statement of Literary Position*

It is also possible to discover certain attitudes which are constant in Stewart's critical writing. He believes that in all the arts, the true function of the artist is not just to make a transcript of life, but to create an image, to set down a vision of life.[22] He refuses to accept art as a "weapon"; rather he reminds us that Aristotle said that the moral good of art is its catharsis in laughter or tears of the troubled spirit of man.[23] He repeatedly stresses the value of humor and comedy in literature. Comedy, he believes, is harder to write than tragedy, and in any case, if realism is the accurate reflection of life, the humorous is more realistic than the gloomy.[24] "Laughter really is the most sensible and serious comment anybody can make on life,"[25] he maintains, and as he demonstrates in the subjects of so many of his poems, he sees the spectacle of man on the earth as "richly comic."[26]

He bitterly opposes literary censorship, and in all his writing life has inveighed against it. As far back as 1948, when censorship in Australia was particularly repressive, he wrote that the law should be changed so the author's *intention* should be examined; this, he felt, was the only tolerable form censorship should take; he was sure that with such an approach, even Joyce's *Ulysses* (which was banned at the time) could be placed "beyond doubt, in the category of the healthy and the profound."[27]

Yet to some, others of his attitudes expressed at the time might have seemed paradoxically illiberal. One of his most positive statements about trends in contemporary literature as he saw them, is contained in a long essay, "Escapes from Art," in *The Flesh and the Spirit*.* Stewart's thesis is that, granted it is the personal responsibility of the artist to fulfill the talent which has been bestowed on him, the problems of contemporary art and the artist are precisely those enunciated by Matthew Arnold in his day—the desire for escape by the rejection of life as it is and escape into one's own personality. Stewart defines the modern equivalents:

Unaltered in spirit in spite of the names we give them, what are the Leftist and the Freudian movements in modern letters but the old deplorable escapes—one rejecting life as men live it, the other borrowing and drowning in the bogs of personality.

(89)

He sees the harm in creative writing caused by Freud's theories as far outweighing any advantages gained in the way of clearer insights into human psychology. He cites W. H. Auden as a poet whose work has been adversely affected by Freudian beliefs:

---

* Page numbers are given after quotations.

"Auden's 'toughness,'" his obscurity and his eschewing of 'poetic' words are the result of the fear and shame with which Freud infected the intellectuals who chose to submit to him" (90). Indeed, Stewart believes, many poets of his time refused to write "naturally on the great traditional themes of love, landscape or heroic action" (93) for the same reasons; and that both the surrender to Freud and the desperate flight from Freud have led, inevitably, to obscurity.

[It] has begotten the most difficult, the most "sophisticated," the most unintelligible art of our time. The vulgar displays of private erudition in "The Waste Land," in Pound's *Cantos* and in Auden's *New Year Letter*; Gertrude Stein's prattling, as of an idiot child; and, worse than any, the escape into a private language as in Joyce's *Finnegans Wake* and the early poems of Dylan Thomas—all these which we find "interesting" are merely, in the aggravated form of unintelligibility, those "allegories of the state of one's own mind" which Matthew Arnold rightly judged to be an escape into inferior art.

(94)

Stewart attacks with equal gusto the "orthodoxy of the Left." He considers that Australian writers are infected too, so that even to question this orthodoxy invites the accusation that one is opposed to any sort of "progress." It must be remembered that Stewart wrote this essay just after World War II. His denunciation of Leftism was thus given specific orientation:

If Leftism was outside war, it was outside life; if it washed its hands of the war, it washed its hands of humanity. If, when mankind was faced with the necessity of accepting heroic values, it had no affirmation to offer, it demonstrated that it had conveyed no genuine illumination in the less dramatic struggle of peace. It had not fought to improve the lot of man, as it professed, but had merely been the plaint of weak spirits against the burden and delight of existence. In plain words, Freudism and Leftism failed mankind in its agony.

(101)

Stewart throughout his critical writing has maintained his stance against obscurity in literature. He objected to the "reduction of the English language to a private mumbo jumbo."[28] Kafka's *The Trial* and Wyndham Lewis's *The Childermas* did not "make sense"[29] to him: closer to home, as it were, he reviewed Patrick White's novel *The Tree of Man* unfavorably because of obscurity of "action and motive."[30] One of the wittiest essays in *The Flesh and the Spirit*, entitled "A Very Joyce Morsel," is a nonetheless devastating attack on *Finnegans Wake* for its obscurity:

When all the ingenuity is recognized, when one has admitted the Rabelaisian humour of the interludes, so nearly making sense, with which the narrative is garnished, the book's real purpose remains ink, remains out of the reader's depth, and the fault lies in the method, not in the reader. . . . Giving Joyce due credit for the magnitude of his conception, wouldn't one get almost exactly the same result from reading the *Encyclopaedia Britannica* backwards?

(44)

In retrospect Stewart now concedes value in poetic innovation; since it is very difficult to say anything new in poetry he appreciates that modern poets "find themselves driven into obscurity and verbal experiment" in their search for freshness.[31]

Stewart values "form" in literature above all else—without form, he maintains, a book is nothing, just as a man is nothing without his inner integrity; as the universe without form would be nothing.[32] He is cautious in his definitions; he deplores, for instance, the use of the word "classic" in too loose a sense: the term should only be applied to, for instance, a novel that could take its place, on its own intrinsic merits, among the great books of the world's literature—otherwise it has no right to that "august description."[33] But this liberal view disguises a leaven of literary chauvinism; he deplored the fact once that Sterne, having written an "odd book," is given full credit for knowing what he was doing; but when the Australian Joseph Furphy wrote an odd book, it was felt that he had "blundered into it." Chekhov writes with "a beautiful simplicity and an exquisite symmetry of form." He is described as a great artist. On the other hand, the Australian short-story writer Henry Lawson achieves the same effect—but he is said to be "artless."[34] Stewart supports the Australian critic A. A. Phillips in his coining of the phrase "cultural cringe"[35]—the Australian habit, or inferiority complex, of undervaluing its writers by comparison with their European equivalents.

Stewart considers that all "movements," except for the "movers," are bad; any writer who borrows someone else's vision instead of being true to his own, imperils his creative genius.[36] It is because of his unshakeable belief in this creed that Stewart venerates the Australian writer and painter Norman Lindsay, whose friendship he enjoyed for over twenty years. "Norman Lindsay," Stewart wrote once, "is the only Australian creative artist who has made of his personal vision of life a new world, a world as wide as the earth we inhabit, and, like the earth, dark or shining with intimations of hell and heaven."[37] But the fact is that in this respect Lindsay is Stewart's examplar, since Stewart himself is true to his own vision and creed.

We see this particularly when we examine Stewart's poetry criticism. He wrote once of his admiration of Hazlitt's precept that a man should first of all speak out simply and plainly, and that these principles should apply no less to poetry than to prose: after all, plainness, directness, and simplicity were closely in accord with Wordsworth's theory and practice, "which brought new life to English poetry after the jewelled clockwork of the eighteenth century," and was furthermore in line with Yeats's insistence for poetry of the use of "the natural words in their natural order."[38] It is for these reasons that Stewart has praised Eliot's poetry: "a verse so clear, so limpid that it becomes like a pane of glass through which may shine the pure poetry of thought and vision."[39] Shelley, similarly, achieved for Stewart an enduring contemporaneousness in his love lyrics—a modernity brought about by "purity of outline and simplicity of imagery."[40] Stewart extends these principles to a logical conclusion when he writes:

When a poet writes about men and their behaviour, he enters into competition with the novelist and the short story writer, and here there are certain elementary rules that he must observe. "Make see," said Conrad; and again, "Wring the last ounce out of your subject."[41]

III *Assessment of His Contemporaries*

It is interesting, then, to see how Stewart applies his theories of poetry in writing about his contemporaries. When Robert D. FitzGerald's long poem "Between Two Tides" appeared in 1952,

Stewart hailed it as "the best long poem that has yet been written in Australia—a poem like this, telling a story, marched
straight into the territory so long left to the novelist"—it was thus
of the utmost importance to Australian poetry. Stewart stressed
that, as long as art was not sacrificed, poetry should appeal to
the widest possible audience. "I have long believed," he concluded, "that it was the turning away from narrative poetry in
Eliot's *Waste Land* and Ezra Pound's *Cantos*, followed by a
general descent into private mysticism that has made poetry in
our time so unpopular with the public, so narrow and meagre an
instrument of civilization."[42]

Underlying his own poetical beliefs was his somewhat astrin-
gent criticism of A. D. Hope's *The Wandering Islands*, a collection of poems that appeared in 1955. Stewart wrote in the "Red
Page" (October 19, 1955):

There is so little freshness in his poetry; so little delight; so little real
contact with life, either in Nature, or, except in his narrow view of
sex, humanity. The form of his verse is limited practically to the
quatrain: his style, though capable of minor variation and of moments
of music, has nothing in the way of subtle, profound and variable
harmony to compare with, for example, Kenneth Slessor's.

Indeed, it is in Slessor's poetry particularly that Stewart has
found great artistic kinship, and two essays on Slessor's poetry
can be numbered among his most noteworthy incursions into
the criticism of poetry and poets. These are "Harbour and
Ocean" in *The Flesh and the Spirit* (pp. 157–63) and "Kenneth
Slessor's Poetry" in *Meanjin Quarterly* (June 1969, pp. 149–68).
He was, of course, a close friend of Slessor, but this, far from
prejudicing his appreciation of Slessor's poetry in its favor, rather
gave him a clearer and more understanding perception of it.

"Harbour and Ocean" is mainly devoted to an analysis and
appreciation of Slessor's now famous poem, "Five Bells." To
illustrate his opinion of its greatness he compares it, as has
been previously noted, to Matthew Arnold's "Thyrsis." And
while he sees nothing in "Five Bells" to match "the melody and
colour of the great conclusion to that poem—the grapes, the
Chianti wine, the green bursting figs, the blue Midland waters
and the dark Iberians"—yet Stewart feels that neither is there in

Arnold's elegy "the profound and tragic music of Slessor's conclusion, that mighty waste of the Harbour, the boat's whistle, and the bells that ring and die." But Stewart would not reach a verdict on the comparisons. He believes poems should be judged, not in isolation, but in relation to a man's whole work: he would not say at that point, therefore, that the reader could know where Slessor stood in the same way as he would know Arnold's stature—"it is much too early." He was prepared to say that Slessor on his published work to that point stood "in the forefront of contemporary Australian writing" and could be assured of "a permanent reputation."

In the latter essay, "Kenneth Slessor's Poetry," Stewart attempted a definitive analysis of the poet's work, realizing that Slessor, not having written poetry since 1942 (the former essay had been written just prior to this), could be regarded as having ended his poetic career (he died one year later). He roamed over Slessor's verse, pointing out key words and phrases which seemed to make his poems "come floating up from his subconscious like bubbles." He noted astonishing feats of observation in Slessor's poetry—such as "Beaches wind-glittering with crumbs of gilt." Who else, marveled this poet of the other, "would look at the sand so closely as to see it grain by grain, as 'crumbs of gilt'? It is a piece of observation that never fails to astonish me."

Stewart's perceptiveness as a poet makes for criticism of the highest order and illumination. Take, for instance, his comments on Slessor's last poem, "Beach Burial." Writing of the stanza

> Dead seamen, gone in search of the same landfall,
> Whether as enemies they fought,
> Or fought with us, or neither; the sand joins them together,
> Enlisted on the other front,

Stewart confesses he had been perturbed by what he thought was the solitary blemish of this "exquisite lament"—the appearance of excessively vague rhyming of "fought" with "front." "But," writes Stewart, "now I realize, what should have been apparent from the first reading, that the true rhyming sequence is 'whether—neither—together—other' and that is quite enough rhyme for any stanza."

So, one's understanding of Slessor's poem is enriched by the acuteness of a poet's observation, as it is also when Stewart tells us that he remarked to Slessor once that he admired his "Captain Dobbin" for having been written in the sort of blank verse that "sang itself into the memory without the slightest difficulty: an extraordinarily difficult feat for blank verse to achieve." Slessor reminded Stewart that Tennyson's "Tears, Idle Tears" had a similar surprise for the reader—and Stewart, always believing it to have been written in rhyme, found to his astonishment that it was not. He attributes the accomplishment of this "miracle" in "Five Bells" to "vowel music, internal rhyme, alliteration and assonance: essentially a tone of voice, the high pure music of threnody."

Stewart, in sum, saw Slessor's best poetry written when he was "inside life, accepting rather than questioning its values"; he saw Slessor as a poet "intensely, tragically, passionately, even furiously aware of the brevity of human life." And after the passage of twenty-seven years or more he was now prepared to make his final judgment of Slessor: "No poet in Australia so far has had more to offer; few, if any, have as much."

IV Versatility as Critic

Stewart in his literary criticism has shown the same astonishing versatility that he displays in his writing at large. During the twenty years of his editorship of the "Red Page" he turned out column after column of appraisal and analysis of writers from Blake, Boswell, Disraeli, Southey, and Shelley to Yeats, E. M. Forster, John Cowper Powys (for whom he has always confessed a great affinity), and to modern poets like Eliot, Auden, and Graves. He has written on practically every Australian writer past and present; among his more memorable judgments can be recalled his remarks on Patrick White's *The Tree of Man*:

... Mr. White writes his bad prose so painstakingly and with such hints of possible excellence that one has no doubts that he could write well if he chose. ... If he has not written the Great Australian novel this time, Mr. White may very well write one of our great novels as soon as he stops trying to.[43]

on Christina Stead (after suggesting influences of Lawrence and Virginia Woolf):

There is a profoundly original talent speaking in *For Love Alone*, something wild and fierce and fearless that tempts one to use the word "genius."[44]

on Eve Langley's *The Pea-Pickers* (a novel which Stewart steadfastly and consistently admires to this day):

Here is the most original contribution to Australian literature since Tom Collins wrote *Such Is Life*; here is a book which is certainly, as A. G. Stephens said cautiously of *Such Is Life*, "an Australian classic"; here, further, is a book which has the qualities of permanent literature and which could take its place beside, say, Keats's letters, in Everyman's Library.[45]

Every one of these opinions, I believe, has been justified during a generation of Australian literary criticism.

But Stewart's versatility as a critic goes even further. He has written knowledgeably and authoritatively on Australian art over the years of his Australian sojourn. He has shown a special interest in the landscape school of Tom Roberts, Streeton, Gruner, Hilder, Lance Solomon, Clifton Pugh, and others. Perhaps his most signal service in art criticism has been to urge a check on the enthusiasm Australians have shown toward so-called primitive painters, especially among the Australian aborigines. The cult of these painters, headed by Albert Namatjira, was for a time very strong in Australia: Stewart's was one of the few voices to counsel a moderation of this enthusiasm. Namatjira, he conceded, would rank as a sensitive and capable water colorist in any company" but he said, of one of Namatjira's disciples, "if Richard Moketarinja is 'amazing,' what is there left to say about Turner?"[46] But his most ironically devastating remarks about the so-called "art of the primitive" are contained in the following passage, which is entitled, as far as Australian art criticism is concerned, to be the final word on the subject:

Primitive man himself certainly never had any doubts as to which culture was superior, his or ours. When Columbus arrived off America in a sailing ship the natives worshipped him as a god. If he had arrived in the *Queen Mary* or a Flying Fortress they would probably have lost their wits with wonder and admiration. When I am told of some ineffable superiority in the bric-a-brac of savage peoples, I recall that these peoples themselves once thought our arts—and the cheapest and meanest of them—so miraculous that they sold us half the world for objects we regarded as despicable trumperies: glass beads and blankets, mirrors and ribbons. The simple African negro had at least the wit to perceive that never during the centuries of his "culture" had he been able to devise a work of art so elegant as the top-hat. He would have felt himself unworthy to enter a temple of such magnificence as the average suburban bungalow. Not even in his dreams had he conceived that there could be shining taps, h. and c. . . . I do not forget that the primitive gentlemen themselves would have climbed high mountains and crossed wide plains to look with awe upon the glory of our average mass-produced floral carpet. And I must remember when I go home tonight that, though justly pleased with the "delicacy of line" of his own works of art, primitive man would have fallen on his knees before the patterned splendour of the lino. on my kitchen floor.[47]

V   *Stewart's Place as Critic*

It is indeed in his creative capacity to produce what one may term critical images that Stewart ranks among the most respected and admired critics of our generation. His felicities of phrasing are likely to be remembered long after the work he is discussing has been forgotten. Thus, discussing a minor Australian novel (*Up the Country*) he writes:

> It reminds you of those inviting bush roads which stride out purposefully into the wilderness as if they had something extremely important at the end of them, and which arrive when you get to the end, nowhere, petering out pleasantly enough, in a sense, in the chaos of gum trees.[48]

Or again, in reviewing John Cowper Powys's *Owen Glendower*:

> [it] is a window through which one sees in even more vivid detail one of the strangest minds of our time.[49]

And when it comes to the ineffable sense of delight mixed with awe that the contemplation of the work of a genius brings, here

again Stewart is able to put this into words with a critical image
that is entirely apposite:

Trying to say the last word on Blake—as critic after critic has attempted to do—is like trying to say the last word on the sunset:
artists can paint it, writers describe it, scientists analyse it, yet evening after evening elusive and inexhaustible in its mystery, the challenge is repeated in the sky.[50]

Trying to say the last word on Stewart as a literary critic is
easier only because he seems to me to conform so admirably to
the requisites so eloquently and definitively put forward by
Dr. Helen Gardner in *The Business of Criticism*: that the critic
sees his primary task as elucidation or illumination, and, this
being the case, "he is concerned with things which are precious
to his readers as well as to himself. His task 'to add sunshine to
daylight, by making the day happier': to help himself and his
readers to understand more deeply and to enjoy more fully what
he and they already understand and enjoy. . . ."[51] Such a critic,
assuredly, is Douglas Stewart.

Conclusion

It is doubtful whether any Australian writer in the last fifty years has had a more profound influence on Australian writing than Douglas Stewart. His monuments, whether in people or published work, surround him. Almost every younger contemporary poet of note owes something to Stewart's personal examples or encouragement; poets of Stewart's generation consistently testify to his literary beneficence, stemming from his *Bulletin* days. Most recently, the poet Rosemary Dobson paid this warmly affectionate and perceptive tribute:

Stewart's influence was far-reaching. As literary editor of the *Bulletin* he published new poetry, and gave encouragement to a variety of talent. He referred many of these poets to publishers, recommending publication of their collections. And on publication he brought the work before the notice of a wide public in his reviews.

It is a strange experience to return to the *Bulletin* of the forties, as I have been doing lately. It was, of course, a completely different paper from the *Bulletin* of today. Its famous opening Red Page was, in fact, at that time Pink, and here Douglas Stewart published every week two or three reviews, with a generous insistence on Australian books. Very often there was a column of verse—one, two or three poems. Appropriately the first poem of the decade was Eve Langley's "Native Born". It became terribly important to be published on that page.[1]

As a poet Stewart has been more consistently prolific and wide-ranging in subject and theme than any of his contemporaries. His has been poetry of story, description and converse, unaffected by trends and fads and yet conveying every quality of singable and memorable verse—flexibility, a delight in phrasing, a range of tone and feeling, and in addition what has been aptly described as "a remarkable and romantic plumpness and warmth of vocabulary."[2] Above all there is a happiness and humor which pervades much of his work, verging onto a gentle

152

irony as the scope of his poetry embraces the most common as well as the most extraordinary things of life about him. Notwithstanding the diversity of his poetic subjects he remains preeminent and unchallenged in his country, perhaps during this century, as a nature poet—his nature lyrics differing from those of his most talented predecessors and contemporaries, as his fellow poet Vivian Smith has so felicitously put it, "in their sparseness of emotion, their drier, more etched tone and in the way they tactfully accept the play of image as an end in itself."[3]

For his versatility, Stewart is unmatched in Australian literature. By exploiting the creative potentialities of radio to communicate culturally, he has established himself internationally as a verse playwright; he ranks among the two or three greatest of Australian literary editors; his literary criticism is consistently respected among his peers; his prose writing, though less fecund as a literary activity, has achieved its own particular permanence in his country's literature. And this versatility has not only been demonstrated in creative output: it has been, no less remarkably, a versatility of creative interests. His love of Australian theater, art, and sculpture, his proselytizing for them during the 1940s, set an example which some of his most distinguished fellow poets duly followed. David Campbell added color to his poetry with an acquired enthusiasm for European painting and aboriginal rock carvings; Francis Webb found music the most important of the other arts, as did James McAuley, along with painting and cartography, and Rosemary Dobson with typography. The renascence since the post–World War II years to the present day of indigenous Australian art and culture, of creative writing and particularly its publishing, in no small part puts contemporary Australia very much in debt to Douglas Stewart—a modest, unassuming, and generous man who would, indeed, be the very last person to concede this.

Notes and References

Chapter One

1. Douglas Stewart, *Australian Writers and Their Works* (Melbourne, 1965), p. 7.
2. *Ibid.*, p. 173.
3. *Ibid.*, p. 13.
4. Douglas Stewart, ed., *Modern Australian Verse* (Sydney, 1968), Introduction pp. xxxii–xxxiv.
5. *Ibid.*, p. xxxiv.
6. "Kenneth Slessor's Poetry," *Meanjin Quarterly*, June 1969, p. 159.
7. "The Humorists," *Collected Poems 1936–1967* (Sydney, 1967), pp. 128–29.
8. Introduction to *The Penguin Book of Australian Verse* (Melbourne, 1972), p. 45.

Chapter Two

1. Tape-recorded interview with Clement Semmler, December 26, 1972 (tape and transcript held in Archives Department of Australian Broadcasting Commission, Sydney). Henceforth referred to as "Recorded Interview."
2. *Ibid.*
3. Introduction to *Douglas Stewart—Selected Poems: Australian Poets Series* (Sydney, 1963), p. v. Stewart quotes the poem.
4. *Ibid.*, p. vi.
5. *The Literature of Australia* (Melbourne, 1964), p. 364.
6. "Douglas Stewart—Lyric Poet," *Meanjin Quarterly*, March 1967, p. 43.
7. *Ibid.*, p. 178.
8. See Note 1, above.
9. See Note 6, above, p. 48.
10. See Note 1, above.
11. *Ibid.*
12. *The Elements of Poetry* (Brisbane, 1963), p. 38.
13. *Ibid.*, p. 40.

14. "Words," in *An Anthology of Modern Verse* (London, 1921), p. 213.

15. *The Literature of Australia*, p. 366.

16. I am indebted for this phrase to Vivian Smith (see Note 6 above).

17. *Ibid.*, p. 44.

18. *The Elements of Poetry*, p. 31.

19. *Douglas Stewart*—Australian Writers and Their Work, Series (Melbourne, 1965), p. 18.

20. *The Literature of Australia*, p. 370.

21. See Note 1. This is an expression Stewart used in this interview.

22. See Note 3, p. vii.

23. *The Elements of Poetry*, p. 33.

24. See Note 3, p. viii.

25. *Ibid.*, p. ix.

26. *The Literature of Australia*, p. 366.

27. See Note 1 for these references.

28. See Note 6, pp. 49–50.

29. Introduction to *Modern Australian Verse* (Sydney, 1964), pp. xxxiii–xxxiv.

30. *Douglas Stewart*, p. 10.

31. "Kenneth Slessor's Poetry," *Meanjin Quarterly*, June 1968, p. 157.

32. See Note 1.

33. *Ibid.*

34. *The Birdsville Track and Other Poems* (Sydney, 1955).

35. *Narrative of an Exploration into Central Australia* (London, 1849), Vol. II, p. 90.

36. *Australian Literature* (London, 1960).

Chapter Three

1. *A History of Australian Literature* (Sydney, 1961), Vol. II, p. 1180.

2. "On Being a Verse Playwright," *Meanjin Quarterly*, September 1964, p. 273.

3. *Prospero and Ariel* (London, 1971), p. 57.

4. Recorded interview.

5. *Ibid.*

6. *The Bulletin*, Red Page, January 3, 1945.

7. *The Bulletin*, Red Page, May 24, 1950.

8. Recorded Interview.

9. *Ibid.*

10. See "The Muse at Mittagong," Sydney *Morning Herald*, December 9, 1967.

11. *The Flesh and the Spirit* (Sydney, 1948), p. 152.

12. "On Being a Verse Playwright," *Meanjin Quarterly*, September 1964, p. 274.

13. Recorded Interview.

14. *Towards an Australian Drama* (Sydney, 1953), p. 134.

15. *Ibid.*, p. 134.

16. *Scott's Last Expedition, Vol. I: The Journals of Captain Scott*, arr. Leonard Huxley (London, 1913), p. 592.

17. "Douglas Stewart," in *The Literature of Australia* (Melbourne, 1964), p. 371.

18. *Towards an Australian Drama*, p. 134.

19. *Douglas Stewart (Australian Writers and Their Work)* (Melbourne, 1965), p. 28.

20. Recorded Interview.

21. *Ibid.*

22. "Shakespeare's Rhythm," *The Bulletin*, Red Page, August 11, 1918.

23. Recorded Interview.

24. *Ibid.*

25. *The Australian Tradition* (Melbourne, 1958), p. 137.

26. Introduction to *Three Australian Plays* (Melbourne, 1963), pp. 15–16).

27. Recorded Interview.

28. *Ibid.*

29. "Douglas Stewart and the Art of the Radio Play," *Texas Quarterly*, Summer 1962, p. 194.

30. Nancy Keesing, *Douglas Stewart* (Melbourne, 1965).

31. *Towards an Australian Drama*, p. 141.

32. *Ibid.*, p. 143.

33. Recorded Interview.

34. *Ibid.*

35. "The Cocktail Party," *The Bulletin*, Red Page, May 24, 1950.

36. Stage directions for *Shipwreck*, Douglas Stewart, *Four Plays* (Sydney, 1958), p. 227.

37. *The Literature of Australia*, p. 374.

38. "An Approach to the Plays of Douglas Stewart," *Southerly*, 1963, No. 2, p. 108.

39. *Douglas Stewart*, p. 30.

40. "Second Thoughts about Douglas Stewart," *Westerly*, 1960, No. 3, p. 27.

41. *Towards an Australian Drama*, p. 144.
42. Recorded Interview. However, the play eventually was broadcast by the ABC on July 7, 1973.
43. *Ibid.*
44. *Douglas Stewart*, p. 30.
45. "Story from Tonga," *The Bulletin*, Red Page, November 5, 1952.
46. "Eliot's New Play," *The Bulletin*, Red Page, May 26, 1954.
47. "The Great Australian Myth," *The Bulletin*, Red Page, August 4, 1943.
48. "Somerset Maugham," *The Bulletin*, Red Page, April 7, 1954.
49. Recorded Interview.
50. Douglas Stewart and Nancy Keesing, ed. *Australian Bush Ballads* (Sydney, 1955), Preface, p. vii.
51. *Ibid.*, p. ix.
52. Recorded Interview.
53. *Ibid.*
54. Keith Macartney, *Fisher's Ghost*, Review in *Meanjin Quarterly*, December 1960, p. 458.
55. *A History of Australian Literature*, Vol. II, p. 1184.

Chapter Four

1. Review in *The Bulletin*, Red Page, December 6, 1944.
2. Douglas Stewart, ed. *Short Stories of Australia* (Sydney, 1967), Introduction, p. viii.
3. See Note 1 above.
4. Recorded Interview.
5. "The Gay Horizon," *The Bulletin*, September 15, 1943.
6. *Short Stories of Australia*, Introduction, p. viii.

Chapter Five

1. George Mackaness and W. W. Stone, eds., *The Books of the Bulletin* (Sydney, 1955), p. 51.
2. Vance Palmer, *The Legend of the Nineties* (Melbourne, 1954), p. 91.
3. The precise date was August 8, 1896. Up till this time the pages had been used for advertisements, mainly of books for sale, although an exception was made when Henry Lawson's *In the Days when the World Was Wide* was reviewed on February 15, 1896.
4. Recorded Interview.
5. *Ibid.*
6. *Ibid.*

7. "The Australian Tradition," *The Bulletin*, Red Page, March 17, 1943.

8. "Three Australian Critics," *The Bulletin*, Red Page, August 14, 1957.

9. "Marcus Clarke," *The Bulletin*, Red Page, October 1, 1958.

10. *"Geoffrey Hamlyn*—An Australian Classic?" *The Bulletin*, Red Page, October 22, 1952.

11. Peter Coleman, in the Foreword to *The Bulletin Books* (Sydney, 1966).

12. *The Legend of the Nineties*, p. 108.

13. Recorded Interview.

14. References quoted from the Preface are on p. x.

15. "A Book of Australian Verse," *The Bulletin*, Red Page, July 18, 1956.

16. Vivian Smith, "Douglas Stewart, Lyric Poet," *Meanjin Quarterly*, March 1967, p. 41.

17. *The Bulletin* at this time (and until the late 1960s) was published with red covers which came to be used for literary articles, poems, and reviews—and were known collectively as the "Red Page."

18. "A. G. Stephens," *The Flesh and the Spirit* (Sydney, 1948), p. 26.

19. "Harbour and Ocean," *The Flesh and the Spirit*, p. 159.

20. *The Bulletin*, Red Page, June 1, 1955.

21. "Not for Gold Medals," *The Bulletin*, Red Page, May 17, 1957.

22. "The Moment of Vision," *The Flesh and the Spirit*, p. 141.

23. "Six Australian Poets," *The Flesh and the Spirit*, p. 72.

24. "The Writing of A. C. Headley," *The Bulletin*, Red Page, February 4, 1942.

25. "In Defence of Arnold Wall," *The Flesh and the Spirit*, p. 115.

26. "The Moment of Vision," *The Bulletin*, Red Page, August 9, 1944.

27. "Answer to Censors," *The Bulletin*, Red Page, February 18, 1948.

28. "Goodbye to the Wreckers," *The Bulletin*, Red Page, October 7, 1942.

29. "On John Cowper Powys's *Owen Glendower*," *The Bulletin*, Red Page, May 20, 1942.

30. "The Tree of Man," *The Bulletin*, Red Page, July 18, 1956.

31. Douglas Stewart, ed., *Modern Australian Verse* (Sydney, 1968), Introduction, p. xxxiv.

32. "Books and the Platypus," *The Flesh and the Spirit*, p. 244.

33. *"Geoffrey Hamlyn*—An Australian Classic?" *The Bulletin,* Red Page, October 22, 1952.

34. "The Australian Tradition," *The Bulletin,* Red Page, May 21, 1958.

35. *Ibid.*

36. "Three Australian Critics," *The Bulletin,* Red Page, August 14, 1957.

37. "An Australian Epic," *The Bulletin,* Red Page, May 19, 1948.

38. "FitzGerald's New Poems," *The Bulletin,* Red Page, December 2, 1953.

39. *Ibid.*

40. "On Shelley," *The Bulletin,* Red Page, April 29, 1942.

41. "Australian Poetry 1944," *The Flesh and the Spirit,* p. 210.

42. "Story from Tonga," *The Bulletin,* Red Page, November 11, 1952.

43. "The Tree of Man," *The Bulletin,* Red Page, July 18, 1956.

44. "Glory and Catastrophe," *The Flesh and the Spirit,* p. 234.

45. "A Letter to Shakespeare," *The Flesh and the Spirit,* p. 31.

46. "Namatjira," *The Bulletin,* Red Page, August 22, 1951.

47. "The Cult of the Primitive," *The Flesh and the Spirit,* p. 8.

48. "Up the Country," *The Bulletin,* Red Page, July 18, 1951.

49. "Owen Glendower," *The Bulletin,* Red Page, May 20, 1942.

50. "On Blake," *The Bulletin,* Red Page, June 17, 1942.

51. *The Business of Criticism* (London, 1959), p. 16.

Conclusion

1. "A World of Difference," *Southerly,* Number Four, December 1973, pp. 373–74.

2. Alec King in "The Look of Australian Poetry in 1967," *Meanjin Quarterly,* June 1968, p. 172.

3. "Douglas Stewart, Lyric Poet," *Meanjin Quarterly,* March 1967, p. 47.

Selected Bibliography

PRIMARY SOURCES
Arranged Chronologically

1. Poems

Green Lions. Auckland: Whitcomb and Tombes, 1936.
The White Cry. London: J. M. Dent, 1939.
Elegy for an Airman. Sydney: Frank C. Johnson, 1940.
Sonnets to the Unknown Soldier. Sydney: Angus and Robertson, 1941.
The Dosser in Springtime. Sydney: Angus and Robertson, 1946.
Glencoe, A Series of Ballads. Sydney: Angus and Robertson, 1947.
Sun Orchids, and Other Poems. Sydney: Angus and Robertson, 1952.
The Birdsville Track, and Other Poems. Sydney: Angus and Robertson, 1955.
The Garden of Ships, A Poem. Sydney: Wentworth Press, 1962.
Rutherford, and Other Poems. Sydney: Angus and Robertson, 1962.
Poems. Selected and Introduced by the Author. Sydney: Angus and Robertson, 1963 (new edition, 1973).
Collected Poems 1936–1967. Sydney: Angus and Robertson, 1967 (comprises most of the poems from previous editions).
Douglas Stewart Reads from His Own Work (gramophone recording with accompanying text of selected poems). Brisbane: University of Queensland Press, 1971.
The Poems of Douglas Stewart. Unscripted narration presented by Douglas Stewart on ABC Radio 2, July 1, 1973. Transcript held by Radio Drama and Features Department of Australian Broadcasting Commission, Sydney.

2. Plays

Ned Kelly. Sydney: Angus and Robertson, 1943. Reprinted 1946. A new edition with an Introduction by the Author, 1961.
The Fire on the Snow and The Golden Lover, Two Plays for Radio. Sydney: Angus and Robertson, 1944.
The Earthquake Shakes the Land. A Radio Drama. Script in Library of Radio Drama and Features Department, Australian Broadcasting Commission, 1944.

161

Shipwreck. Sydney: The Shepherd Press, 1947.

The Fire on the Snow, with an Introduction by the Author. Sydney: Angus and Robertson, 1954 (frequently re-printed).

Four Plays (*The Fire on the Snow, The Golden Lover, Ned Kelly, and Shipwreck*). Sydney: Angus and Robertson, 1958.

Fisher's Ghost, An Historical Comedy. Sydney: Wentworth Press, 1960.

The Golden Lover, with an Introduction by the Author. Sydney: Angus and Robertson, 1962.

3. Prose Works

A Girl with Red Hair. Sydney: Angus and Robertson, 1944. Short stories.

The Flesh and the Spirit. Sydney: Angus and Robertson, 1948. Literary criticism.

The Seven Rivers. Illustrated by Margaret Coen. Sydney: Angus and Robertson, 1966. Ostensibly on his experiences in trout-fishing in New Zealand and Australia, but providing incidentally a fund of personal and autobiographical detail.

4. As Editor

Australian Bush Ballads (with Nancy Keesing as coeditor). Sydney: Angus and Robertson, 1955. Has an excellent Introduction which gives an outline of the development of the Australian ballad, and in which Stewart offers his own theories about its origins.

Old Bush Songs and Rhymes of Colonial Times (with Nancy Keesing as coeditor). Sydney: Angus and Robertson, 1957.

Modern Australian Verse. Sydney: Angus and Robertson, 1964. Has a lively Introduction on the state of Australian poetry. The same text was published by the University of California Press, Berkeley, 1965.

Hugh McCrae: Selected Poems. Sydney: Angus and Robertson, 1966. Has a critical Introduction which assesses McCrae's poetry.

The Pacific Book of Bush Ballads (with Nancy Keesing as coeditor). Sydney: Angus and Robertson, 1967.

Short Stories of Australia: The Lawson Tradition. Sydney: Angus and Robertson, 1967. Has a short Introduction, evaluating the work of the writers chosen.

The Wide Brown Land: A New Selection of Australian Verse. Sydney: Angus and Robertson, 1971.

5. Articles, Interviews, etc.

Introduction to *Fair Girls and Grey Horses*. Sydney: Angus and Robertson, 1958. This discusses the poetry of Will Ogilvie, whose collected verse, mainly in ballad form, this volume comprises.

"Poetry as a Playwright's Craft," *Theatregoer*, March 1962, pp. 14–15.

"On Being a Verse Playwright," *Meanjin Quarterly*, September 1964, pp. 272–77.

Introduction to *Ship Models* by Norman Lindsay. Sydney: Angus and Robertson, 1966.

"Kenneth Slessor's Poetry," *Meanjin Quarterly*, June 1969, pp. 149–68.

Interview with Clement Semmler, December 28, 1972. Transcript in Archives Department, Australian Broadcasting Commission, Sydney.

SECONDARY SOURCES

BRADLEY, DAVID. "Second Thoughts about Douglas Stewart," *Westerly* (1960, No. 3), pp. 23–27.

BURROWS, J. F. "An Approach to the Plays of Douglas Stewart," *Southerly* (1963, No. 2).

BURTON, MARJORIE. "A Guide to *The Fire on the Snow*." Sydney: Jacaranda, 1965 (in "Understanding Literature" series).

FITZGERALD, R. D. *The Elements of Poetry*. St. Lucia: University of Queensland Press, 1963: "Motif in the Work of Douglas Stewart," pp. 25–50. A valuable study by a poet-contemporary.

GREEN, H. M. *A History of Australian Literature*. Sydney: Angus and Robertson, 1961, pp. 258–61 (poetry); 1179–84 (plays); 1203–7 (critical works); 980 (war poems); 1401 (works published after closing date of main text).

HADGRAFT, CECIL. *Australian Literature*. London: Heinemann, 1960, pp. 177–81 (poetry); 285–86 (critical works).

KEESING, NANCY. "Douglas Stewart." Melbourne: Lansdowne, 1965. The most comprehensive study of Stewart's writing to date—a 43-page pamphlet in the "Australian Writers and Their Work" series.

KRESNER, H. A. "Notes on *The Fire on the Snow*." Sydney: Horwitz-Grahame, 1963.

LAWSON, MAX. "A Companion to Douglas Stewart: *Ned Kelly*." Sydney: Angus and Robertson, 1965.

164 DOUGLAS STEWART

MACARTNEY, KEITH. Review of *The Fire on the Snow* and *The Golden Lover, Meanjin Quarterly* (March 1945), pp. 65–67.

MCAULEY, JAMES. "Douglas Stewart," *The Literature of Australia*, ed. G. Dutton. Melbourne: Penguin Books, 1964, pp. 362–76. Another valuable study by a fellow poet.

MILLER, E. MORRIS and MACARTNEY, F. T. *Australian Literature*. Sydney: Angus and Robertson, 1956, pp. 447–48.

OLIVER, H. J. "Douglas Stewart and the Art of the Radio Play," *Texas Quarterly* (Summer 1962), pp. 193–203.

PHILLIPS, A. A. "Douglas Stewart's *Ned Kelly* and Australian Romanticism," *Meanjin Quarterly*, (September 1956), pp. 260–71.

REES, LESLIE. "*Ned Kelly* and Australian Verse Drama," *The Bulletin*, Red Page (March 3, 1943).

———. *Towards an Australian Drama*. Sydney: Angus and Robertson, 1953, pp. 133–45.

SMITH, VIVIAN. "Douglas Stewart, Lyric Poet," *Meanjin Quarterly* (March 1967). A younger contemporary poet's analysis of Stewart's poetry.

OTHER SOURCES

BARNES, JOHN, ED. *The Writer in Australia*. A Collection of Literary Documents 1856–1964. Melbourne: Oxford University Press, 1969.

BUCKLEY, VINCENT. *Essays in Poetry, Mainly Australian*. Melbourne: Melbourne University Press, 1957.

DUTTON, G., ED. *The Literature of Australia*. Melbourne: Penguin Books, 1964. In particular, "Australian Poetry to 1920" by Judith Wright and "Australian Poetry since 1920" by Evan Jones.

ELLIOTT, BRIAN. *The Landscape of Australian Poetry*. Melbourne: Cheshire, 1967.

EWERS, J. K. *Creative Writing in Australia*. Melbourne: Georgian House, 1945 (revised edition, 1962).

HESELTINE, H. P., ED. *The Penguin Book of Australian Verse*. Melbourne: Penguin Books, 1972.

JAFFA, HERBERT C. *Kenneth Slessor*. New York: Twayne Publishers, Inc., 1971.

LAVATER, L. *The Sonnets of Australia—A Survey and Selection*. Sydney: Angus and Robertson, 1956.

LINDSAY, PHILIP. "The Voice of Australia," *Southerly* (1948, No. 3).

MCAULEY, JAMES. *The Personal Elements in Australian Poetry*. Sydney: Angus and Robertson, 1970.

MOORE, T. INGLIS. *Social Patterns in Australian Literature.* Sydney: Angus and Robertson, 1971. A most useful survey of the relation of Australia's literature to its social and political development.

PALMER, VANCE. *The Legend of the Nineties.* Melbourne: Melbourne University Press, 1954.

PHILLIPS, A. A. *The Australian Tradition.* Melbourne: Cheshire, 1958.

SERLE, GEOFFREY. *From the Deserts the Prophets Come*: The Creative Spirit in Australia 1788–1972. Melbourne: Heinemann, 1973. This is perhaps the most important Australian study of its kind written to date.

SEMMLER, CLEMENT AND WHITELOCK, DEREK, EDS. *Literary Australia.* Melbourne: Cheshire, 1966.

SEMMLER, CLEMENT. "Poetry of the 1960s," in *The Art of Brian James and Other Essays in Australian Literature.* St. Lucia: University of Queensland Press, 1972.

SEMMLER, CLEMENT, ED. *Twentieth Century Australian Literary Criticism.* Melbourne: Oxford University Press, 1967.

TORY, ALAN. *Harbour in Heaven.* Sydney: G. M. Dash, 1949.

TULIP, JAMES. "Contemporary Australian Poetry," *Southerly* (1972, No. 2).

WILKES, G. A. and REID, J. C. *The Literatures of the British Commonwealth Series—Australia and New Zealand.* Pennsylvania State University Press, 1970.

WRIGHT, JUDITH. *Preoccupations in Australian Poetry.* Melbourne: Oxford University Press, 1965. A stimulating series of essays by one of Stewart's most formidable contemporaries.

In addition to special articles mentioned above, the files of the Australian literary journals *Meanjin Quarterly* (Melbourne), *Southerly* (Sydney), *Australian Literary Studies* (Hobart), *Overland* (Melbourne), and *Westerly* (Perth) contain much important material relevant to the scope of this study.

Index

A.B.C. *See* Australian Broadcasting Commission

Amundsen, Roald, 67, 73

Anderson, Hugh, 134

Archibald, J. F., 129-30

Auden, W. H., 62, 132, 142-43

Australian Broadcasting Commission (A.B.C.), 19, 59, 64, 68, 87, 95, 101

Australian Literary Studies, 155-65 *passim*

Australian Women's Mirror, 22

Barnes, John, 164

Bates, Daisy, 131

Baynton, Barbara, 130

B.B.C. *See* British Broadcasting Corporation

Becke, Louis, 130

Bedford, Randolph, 130

Blake, William, 150

Blight, John, 134

Boake, Barcroft, 130, 136

Boyd, Arthur, 20

Bradbrook, Muriel, 115

Bradley, David, 101, 160

Brady, E. J., 130, 137

Bridson, D. G., 60, 61

British Broadcasting Corporation (B.B.C.), 60, 62, 68

Buckley, Vincent, 133, 164

Bulletin, 15, 16, 17, 19, 20, 22, 114, 119, 120, 129-36, 140, 152, 155-65 *passim*

Bulletin, Stewart's Editorship of "Red Page," 131-35

Burrows, J. F., 162

Burton, Marjorie, 163

Buzo, Alex, 113

Campbell, David, 21, 32, 132, 134, 153

Campbell, Roy, 26, 47, 52

Canadian Broadcasting Corporation (C.B.C.), 61-62

C.B.C. *See* Canadian Broadcasting Corporation

Cherry-Garrard, Apsley, 68

Clarke, Frances, 133, 159

Coast to Coast, 114, 122, 136

Coen, Margaret (Mrs. Douglas Stewart), 19

Coleman, Peter, 159n11

"Collins, Tom." *See* Furphy, Joseph

Conrad, Joseph, 145

Cowan, James, 87

Daley, Victor, 130

Davis, Arthur Hoey ("Steele Rudd"), 130, 135

Davis, Beatrice, 136

Davison, Frank Dalby, 132, 134

Dobell, William, 20

Dobson, Rosemary, 21, 131, 134, 152, 153

Drysdale, Russell, 20

Dutton, Geoffrey, 164

Dyson, Edward, 130

Eliot, T. S., 62, 63, 103, 132, 145, 146

Elliott, Brian, 133, 164

Ellis, M. H., 133

Ewers, J. K., 164

Finnegans Wake (Joyce), 143-44

FitzGerald, R. D., 15, 17, 21, 27-28, 35, 42, 54, 132, 134, 145, 160, 163

FitzHenry, W. E., 133

Flecker, James Elroy, 60
For the Term of his Natural Life (Clarke), 133
Forshaw, Thelma, 134
Franklin, Miles, 121
Freud, Sigmund, 142-43
Frost, Robert, 132
Fry, Christopher, 62
Furphy, Joseph ("Tom Collins"), 130, 133, 144, 149

Gardner, Helen, 151
Geoffrey Hamlyn (Kingsley), 133
Gilmore, Mary, 131-32, 134
Gordon, Adam Lindsay, 136-37
Graves, Robert, 19
Green, H. M., 59, 113, 163
Gruner, E., 149

Hadcraft, Cecil, 57, 163
Hart-Smith, William, 21, 134
Harte, Bret, 137
Herrick, George, 137
Heseltine, H. P., 21, 164
Hilder, J. J., 149
Hope, A. D., 15, 21, 54, 57, 132, 146
Huxley, Aldous, 132
Huxley, Leonard, 68

Jaffa, Herbert, 164
"James, Brian." *See* Tierney, John
Joyce, James, 120, 122, 142-44

Kafka, Franz, 143
Keesing, Nancy, 15, 17, 35, 50, 80, 101-102, 133, 136, 158n50, 163
Kendall, Henry, 32
King, Alex, 160n2
Kingsley, Henry, 133
Kipling, Rudyard, 137
Kippax, H. G., 86
Kresner, H. A., 163

Lane, William, 46
Langley, Eve, 149, 152
Lavater, Louis, 164

Lawler, Ray, 113
Lawson, Henry, 109, 130, 136, 139-40, 144, 158n3
Lawson, Max, 163
Lewis, C. Day, 132
Lewis, Wyndham, 143
Lindsay, Norman, 17, 19, 27, 133-34, 144, 163
Lindsay, Philip, 164
Literature in Action (Bradbrook), 115

Macartney, F. T., 164
Macartney, Keith, 112, 158n54, 164
McAuley, James, 15, 21, 23, 30, 36, 47, 75, 134, 153, 164
McCrae, Hugh, 17, 134, 137-38, 162
McCuaig, Ronald, 17, 133
Mackaness, George, 158n1
Mackenzie, Kenneth, 17
MacLeish, Archibald, 61
MacNeice, Louis, 61
Mann, Cecil, 17, 131, 134
Mann, Thomas, 132
Mawson, Sir Douglas, 66-67
Meanjin Quarterly, 21, 131, 134, 146, 155-65 *passim*
Miller, E. Morris, 164
Moore, T. Inglis, 165

Namatjira, Albert, 149, 160n46
Neilson, John Shaw, 32

O'Brien, John, 137
O'Casey, Sean, 60
Ogilvie, Will, 137, 163
Oliver, Harold, 88, 164
On Our Selection (Davis), 130
Overland, 155-65 *passim*

Palmer, Vance, 134-35, 158n2, 165
Park, Mungo, 46
Paterson, A. B. ("Banjo"), 109, 130, 136-37
Pelsart, Francis, 60, 100, 101
Phillips, A. A., 85, 132, 144, 164-65
Pound, Ezra, 143, 146

Powys, John Cowper, 26, 108, 132, 148, 150, 159n29
Prix Italia, 62
Pugh, Clifton, 149

Quinn, Roderick, 137

Schlunke, E. O., 132, 134
Scott, Captain Robert, 59, 67
Scott, Sir Walter, 46
Semmler, Clement, 155n1, 163, 165
Serle, Geoffrey, 15, 165
Shackleton, Sir Ernest, 44-45
Shelley, Percy Bysshe, 60, 145
Slessor, Kenneth, 17, 18, 21, 54, 63, 132, 146-47, 155n6, 163
Smith, Vivian, 24, 33, 48, 153, 156-n16, 164
Southerly, 21, 131, 134, 155-65 *passim*
Spender, Stephen, 132
Stead, Christina, 132
Stein, Gertrude, 143
Stephens, A. G., 129-30, 135, 140-41, 149
Stewart, Douglas: approach to poetry, 18; birthplace and date, 16; critic, 140-51; editorship of *Bulletin*'s "Red Page," 131-35; education, 16; poetry, types of—humorous 47-51, love 51-53, meditative 33-40, narrative 40-47, nature 24-33; short story writer, 115-24; verse playwright, 59-112

WORKS: ANTHOLOGIES
Australian Bush Ballads, 135-37
Australian Poetry, 136
Modern Australian Verse, 139
Old Bush Songs, 135-36
Short Stories of Australia, 139

WORKS: CRITICISM
Flesh and the Spirit, The, 140-46

WORKS: POETRY
"Bill Posters," 51
"Bishop, The," 47-48
"Blazes Well," 55

"Branding Fire, The," 58
"Bunyip, The," 54
"Child and Lion," 41
"Christmas Bells," 33
"Cicada Song," 30-31
"Country Song, A," 30
"Day and Night with Snow," 34
"Died in Harness," 34
"Elegy for an Airman," 35
"Fence," 38
"Flock of Gang-Gangs," 31-32
"Four-Letter Words," 49-50
"Glencoe," 41-44
"Goldfish," 28
"Grasshopper," 27
"Green Centipede, The," 26-27
"Heaven is a Busy Place," 51
"Horse," 39
"Humorists, The," 20
"Marree," 56
"Mirror, The," 52-53
"Morning in Wellington," 25
"Mungo Park," 46-47
"Night Camp," 57
"Putorino the Magic Flute," 22-23
"Reflections at a Parking Meter," 48-49
"River, The," 35-36
"Rutherford," 36-38
"Silkworms, The," 39-40
"Stolen Mountain, The," 41
"Stream and Shadows," 29-30
"Summer Dusk, A," 53
"Sunshower," 31
"Terra Australis," 46
"Track Begins, The," 55-56
"Two Englishmen," 57
"Wasp," 29
"Waterlily," 28, 33
"Winter-Crazed, The," 34
"With a Sheaf of Cream Roses," 5, 52
"Worsley Enchanted," 44-45

WORKS: PROSE
Seven Rivers, The, 124-28

WORKS: SHORT STORIES
"Carnival," 120-22

"Girl with Red Hair, A," 115-17

Girl with Red Hair, A (Collection), 114

"Give us This Day," 118-19

"He's Going to Use That Scythe," 118

"Medium, The," 122

"Three Jolly Foxes, The," 122-24

"Whare, The," 117-18

WORKS: VERSE-DRAMA

"Earthquake Shakes the Land, The," 59-60, 95-100

"Fire on the Snow, The," 59, 62-78, 81-82, 87

"Fisher's Ghost," 60, 108-12

"Golden Lover, The," 59, 87-95, 101, 107-108

"Ned Kelly," 59, 65, 78-87, 101, 103, 107

"Shipwreck," 60, 87, 100-108

Stone, W. W., 133, 158n1

Sturt, Captain Charles, 55, 66

Such is Life (Furphy), 130, 133

Tennyson, Alfred (Lord), 148

Thomas, Dylan, 61, 143

Thomas, Edward, 29

Tierney, John ("Brian James"), 131-32, 134

Tory, Alan, 165

Trist, Margaret, 134

Tucker, Albert, 20

Tulip, James, 165

Ulysses (Joyce), 142

Wall, Arnold, 134

Webb, Francis, 131-32, 134, 153

Westerly, 155-65 *passim*

White, Patrick 132, 144, 148

Whitelock, Derek, 165

Wilkes, G. A., 165

Williamson, David, 113

Wordsworth, William, 28, 145

Wright, Judith, 15, 21, 32, 54, 57, 131-32, 134, 165

Yeats, W. B., 23, 60, 94, 145